√C+H

1-16-62   54-8626

THE American People
IN THE TWENTIETH CENTURY

THE LIBRARY OF CONGRESS SERIES
IN AMERICAN CIVILIZATION
EDITED BY RALPH HENRY GABRIEL

THE

American People

IN THE TWENTIETH CENTURY

By Oscar Handlin

HARVARD UNIVERSITY PRESS · CAMBRIDGE

1954

LIBRARY OF CONGRESS CATALOG CARD NUMBER 54–8626

PRINTED IN THE UNITED STATES OF AMERICA

FOR DAVID

FOREWORD

The eighteenth- or nineteenth-century traveler to the United States was often impressed with the flat uniformity of the population he encountered. By contrast with what had been familiar in Europe, all men here looked monotonously alike.

This illusion was the product of the absence in America of the kind of differences familiar to the Old World. Europeans missed here the overt indications of rank. To those accustomed to recognize the occupation, the legally established status, and the antecedents of any individual by his dress, bearing, and speech, Americans seemed cut from one cloth. Except for the persistent distinction between the slave and the freeman, there was no equivalent here of the separateness of classes entrenched across the Atlantic by the force of law and custom.

The uniformity was not real however; had it been so, the task of this volume would have been simpler. It might then have been possible to describe the American people by counting them, as the census does, and by setting forth their general characteristics in terms of the political subdivisions and the large categories of age and sex into which the integers of population fell.

But Americans were not simply integers, all of a kind. The more perceptive voyagers to the New World also early commented upon the striking diversities that set some Americans off from their fellows. Not even in politics were the residents of this country simply undifferentiated units, with one citizen, one vote, like any other. In their labor, in their worship, in their government, in their family life, these people did not fall into monolithic organizations defined by statute or tradition; they found it necessary and convenient instead to express themselves through modes of action not at all uniform and constantly changing. In this society, precisely because few institutions established by law stood in their way, men were free to join one another in what groups they wished, to establish voluntarily what patterns of activity their hearts desired. Fredrika Bremer perceiving the result of that ability in 1840 exclaimed, "These people associate as freely as they breathe." [1]

The variety of the associational groups within which men arranged their lives reflected the variety of the men themselves. Through the history of the United States two main factors determined the differences among Americans and therefore the differences in their affiliation. The great territorial extent of the country and the variations in physiography, in climate, and in form of settlement created sectional distinctions already recognized and described in the eighteenth century, and since then the frequent subjects of investigation by historians.

But intermeshed with the influence of the section was the influence of the variety of antecedents that men carried with them to the place they settled.

Unceasing mobility brought together Americans and those becoming Americans who had been reared in the most dissimilar places and born into the most dissimilar families. These ethnic antecedents produced a variety of people and groups that added complexity to the diversities of sectionalism.

It was a further condition of the freedom and fluidity of life in the United States that such groups rarely acquired the rigidity to keep them long apart from the currents of changes that again and again transformed the nation. Completely voluntary in their membership, without any status in law, they could not maintain themselves once they had outlived their usefulness or ceased to serve the functions that had called them into being. The constant expansion of the nation, socially as well as territorially, was a continual source of instability that not only shifted individuals from one group to another, but also often altered the very structure of the groups themselves.

Therein lies the significance of the period with which the present volume is concerned. At its opening, the general conditions of American growth persisted in much the same form as in the nineteenth century. But, in this portentous half century, the nation passed through a succession of radical transformations. Two world wars, a prolonged depression, a shift in the emphasis of the economy, the development of the media of a mass national culture, and the ending of the era of free immigration exerted a profound influence on the whole of the American population and on the groups which were organized within it. A study of the developments of this period may throw light on the history of the American population, on the evolution of the forms of group action, and on the trends from which the patterns of the future will emerge.

Completion of this volume presents me with yet another occasion for acknowledging my indebtedness to Mary Flug Handlin for unfailing coöperation. Every page of this book has profited from her labors and her thinking.

I am grateful also to the editor of this series, Ralph H. Gabriel, for many helpful comments and for a very careful reading of the text. In the preparation of this book, I have drawn freely upon the splendid resources of the Harvard College Library; and I have been the gainer by the research and discussions in successive seminars at Harvard University on "The Immigrant in American History." I am particularly obliged to Dr. Barbara M. Solomon for assistance with this material. Esther Berger was most helpful when most needed; and Nancy D. Hibbard prepared the manuscript with patience and efficiency.

OSCAR HANDLIN

Harvard University

CONTENTS

A HERITAGE OF EXPANSION

CHAPTER I

A New Century's Vistas

The pessimists hid their heads at the opening of the new century. In their secret hearts, the few who held the views of Henry Adams cherished gloomy doubts concerning the future of civilization in the United States. But even among those few there was little inclination to express in public their forebodings; Indian Summer, decadence, those were terms they whispered among themselves. The audience would be meager indeed for any prophet whose message included quibbling doubts as to whether the growth of the past would continue on into the indefinite future.

The memories of most Americans were still vivid with impressions of the great Chicago exposition of 1893, impressions that would be refreshed in St. Louis in 1904. Twenty-seven million visitors at the first and twenty million more at the second had surveyed with pride the record of their progress. The milling throngs had nothing but impatience for the suggestion that the country had passed its peak. At both expositions curious ongazers had seen visible decisive evidence. For an age disposed to measure progress in terms of the abundance of material things, here were the signs of monumental achievements. The complex rearing machines, black in their iron castings, embodied the power to create goods the like of which man had never before dreamed of owning. The electric light, a novelty in Chicago, was already commonplace in St.

Louis where attention drifted rather to the new horseless car-
riage. And these were objects not merely to be admired, but
to be possessed. The hulking shapes made to labor for man's
enjoyment were symbols of industrial prowess. American output had already outstripped that of every rival and was growing still, at a rate faster than in any other nation in the world.

The sinews of the Western giant did not flex with the
power of manufacturing alone. Its limitless resources of min-
erals and oil confirmed the certainty of continuing preëminence. It was not only that the exciting news from the Klon-
dike held out hope of quick wealth for the venturesome. Other
measures of expanded production for the last decade of the
nineteenth century were still more decisive: Pennsylvania anthracite, up 24 per cent; bituminous coal, up 91 per cent;
iron ore, up 68 per cent; copper, up 135 per cent; and the
relative newcomer, primary aluminum, up 7,605 per cent.
Not many could recite the figures; but everyone knew, vi-
cariously at least, the thrill of discovery as the fluid gold was
released in strike after strike at the wells of Kansas, Texas,
Louisiana, and Oklahoma. Shortly, the amazing Spindletop
Gusher would lead America into the modern oil age.

The revived prosperity of the farms was conclusive. The
industrial cities of America could wither, a spokesman for the
farmers had boasted, but the great agricultural heart of America would continue to beat. Why, what were Chicago, St.
Louis, and New Orleans, even New York and Philadelphia
and San Francisco, but the channels through which moved
that vast outpouring — billions of bushels of wheat, hundreds
of millions of bushels of corn and oats, billions of bales of
cotton, that fed and clothed not this nation alone, but a good
part of the civilized world! Although the percentage of those
engaged in agriculture was falling, technological progress kept
lifting the total output, and, perhaps as important, kept increasing the amenities of life on the farm.

Pride in growth, confidence in the potentiality of further

growth, dulled the edge of any doubt evoked by those in-
stances in the past when economic expansion had slackened.
The panic of 1893 and the miseries of 1894 had receded from
men's consciousness. It seemed now as if the warnings of Bellamy and George and their fellows in reform had been need-
lessly shrill; these occasional depressions were only the immediate means of adjusting the productive machine to enable it
to function more efficiently. There had been no significant
territorial addition to the size of the nation since 1850 (the
overseas territories taken from Spain, whose future was still
being debated, were not reckoned such). Nevertheless, the
country had thrived, since the days of its first settlement, by
an unslackening rise in population. Americans were now
76,000,000 strong, high among the peoples of the earth. In
numbers, they had long since outstripped England and every
other European power. Looking back at the past they were
often amazed at the dizzy pace at which the climb had come.
Only a century earlier they had counted a mere 5,000,000; in
1850, but 23,000,000. This growth, fifteen-fold in a century,
amply justified the certitude of still greater things to come.

Yet, beneath the bustle that expressed all these confident
expectations, there could already be discerned tendencies that
would complicate the process of growth in the half century to
come. The promise of new development was still valid, but
nevertheless there were clear indications that it would take
unforeseen forms.

If there was evidence that the United States as a whole
could be certain of its powers of growth, the same evidence
also showed that some parts of the nation were expanding
more rapidly than others. Through the century that had
closed the center of population had moved steadily westward,
had crossed into Ohio by the time of the Civil War, and had
reached into Indiana by 1890. In 1900, it was already half-
way across the last-named state. This progression reflected the
attractive power of the newly opened areas of settlement.

When the twentieth century began, the whole region beyond the Mississippi had felt the impact of the restless movement toward the Pacific.

Internal population shifts of another sort had almost as long a history. For some seventy years the percentage of Americans who lived in urban places had risen. The 10 per cent who lived in cities in 1830 had become almost 40 per cent in 1900. Furthermore, the trend was toward ever larger units. In 1830, only the 200,000 residents of New York City knew what it was to make homes in a place of more than 100,000 population; seventy years later 14,000,000 Americans in thirty-eight different communities shared that knowledge. As late as 1870, only two municipalities had moved above the half-million mark; in 1900, there were six in that situation, with Chicago and Philadelphia above a million and New York above three. In addition, the aggressive rise of such new towns as Detroit, Los Angeles, and Cleveland gave unmistakable indications that the peak of urbanization had not yet been reached.

These developments had been independent of changes in the birth rate. There were places, as in the southeastern states, where a high fertility rate enabled the native population more than to replace itself. But, taking the United States as a whole, the birth rate seems to have been falling through the nineteenth century; certainly the number of children relative to total population had declined steadily. What was more, the decline had been particularly marked in the very cities that nonetheless continued to grow in total numbers.

The residents of the urban places probably did not reproduce themselves. But that failure also created the conditions that attracted population from other sources and more than compensated. The falling birth rate was a measure of control over the milieu. The curtailment in family size was voluntary, motivated by the desire to improve standards of living. Such limitation, given the expansive trends of commerce and industry, made room for outsiders. For the farm boy, the nearby city was equally the frontier with the opening West.

Furthermore, through the nineteenth century a momentous mass movement brought from across the Atlantic the future citizens who made up for the unborn babes of those long settled in the land.

The Americans of 1900, looking back, could make out two such waves of immigration in their recent past; looking ahead, they could discern a third just beginning. It was not only the learned familiar with statistics who knew the magnitude of those movements. The line of debarking newcomers was now a familiar sight in the United States and every man could see in the teeming cities, in the busy factories, in the acres of new land under cultivation, evidence of the impact of immigration.

Few ever gave a thought to the forces that had set these wanderers in motion. The ultimate source of the movement was a deep-reaching disturbance in the social and economic structure of the Old World. The great transformations of European agriculture and industry that began at the end of the eighteenth century had dislodged from fixed places in fixed societies millions of men for whom there was no longer room where they were. As the old communal forms of village agriculture in Europe gave way to the newer commercial farming, as the old handicraft workshops disappeared in the face of the overwhelming efficiency of the factory, the peasants and artisans who had supplied the labor of the old order found themselves displaced. The continent had already discovered the difficulty of supporting a population that increased beyond any precedent; it now had no hope at all for these men. Set on the move, they sought a refuge in the New World.

Almost as soon as the peace of 1815 quieted the disturbances of the turbulent Napoleonic era, the displaced had begun to come. The process had long been in preparation. In its initial stages, its consequences were already felt in America. But the full impact came as the nineteenth century unfolded and year after year that impact increased in cumulative effect. The earliest wave mounted slowly. At first it was largely the more prosperous farmers and artisans who managed to make the crossing. But as time went on a larger emigrating population also found the way, as the poorer peasants joined the movement. By the 1840's the annual number of immigrants was in the hundred thousands. And a series of famines and crop failures after 1846 pushed that number over 200,000 in each of the years between 1847 and 1857, with a peak of more than 400,000 in 1854. In this first wave, the chief sources were England, southwest Germany, and Ireland, although there were also scatterings from other parts of the continent.

Late in the 1860's a second wave took form. Composed of people displaced by the same forces as earlier, this movement however drew upon a wider area of the continent. There were still very large numbers of Englishmen, Irishmen, and Germans on the way; but these were now joined by a mass of Scandinavians set loose by the new economy of the peninsula. And, toward the end of the century, the procession swelled still further with the addition of a conglomerate host of newcomers from eastern Europe as the Austrian and Russian empires in their turn shook under the pressure of change.

In size, the second migration was of an altogether different order from the first. In the first wave, the annual number of entrants exceeded 400,000 only once; the second wave attained that figure in fifteen of its thirty-five years, and reached a peak of almost 800,000 in 1882.

The difference in the magnitude of the two movements originated partly in the fact that the second was cumulative, took in many individuals originally set in motion decades earlier. Here and there were peasants deprived of their land years ago, but unwilling to leave the country of their birth. Perhaps they worked in the factories of nearby cities or toiled as laborers for the gentry, until some more fortunate cousin or uncle from across the Atlantic sent on the redeeming ticket.

Through the century, scores of former villagers, or their sons, were in this manner being regathered in the New World.

Improvements in the means of transportation also stimulated the movement in the last third of the century. The spread of the railway network through Europe made the land journey easier. And the conquest of transatlantic trade by steam navigation softened the incredible tribulations of the old sailing ship voyage. It was now possible to make the entire crossing in a matter of weeks, not months, and in steerage at a relatively low cost. There were still hardships, of course, but fewer than before; that fact not only induced more to come, it enabled more to survive the ordeal.

The course of immigration had added substantially to the population of the United States. Fully 19,000,000 newcomers had entered the country between 1821 and 1900. What part of the total these people and all their descendants constituted by the end of the century is difficult to ascertain. But the census of 1900 revealed that one-third of the nation then consisted of the foreign-born or the children of the foreign-born.

The contribution of numbers was, however, by no means the full extent of the immigrants' influence. They had as well a powerful effect upon the American economy.

Not many had gone to the soil; few possessed the means to make their way beyond the ports where they had first come to rest and to establish themselves as independent farmers. But those who had brought with them the liberating capital, or who had managed to accumulate it once in the United States, significantly affected the westward move of settlement.

Following upon the heels of the frontiersman, the European enabled the original settlers to shift to ever newer frontiers. The American, wasteful as a farmer, inclined to an easy mining of the land, and impatient with the duller labors of cultivation, found himself often in debt and welcomed the newcomers willing to buy his plot at a good price. The immigrants, not themselves prepared to fight the wilderness, lacked the pioneer's experience in clearing the forest or in living off its game. They preferred to purchase in areas already opened up, to labor hard on the soil in which the native had already lost interest. The newcomers, constantly adding capital to agriculture, thus released the frontiersmen to fresh conquests. Together these people subjected to settlement the vast interior areas of the United States.

Although many more among the immigrants longed for the dignity and security of the farmer's position, they were not able to attain it. Too poor to begin with or impoverished on the way, they were unable to get out of the cities. Stranded in the ports of landing or at the interior transfer points, they made what adjustments they could to urban life. Lacking usable skills, the overwhelming majority became laborers. They accumulated in a vast pool of surplus hands available for the needs of the expanding American economy. Unskilled laborers supplied the power for the monumental tasks of construction. Unaided by machines, the newcomers laid millions of miles of streets, railroads, and canals. They built the cities and supplied them with the structures for residence and trade, with the gas, water, and electricity essential to the complex life of these places. These efforts effected a gigantic revolution in transport and in urbanization.

The existence of a reserve of labor ready and willing to work at almost any rate of pay also stimulated industry. The fluid supply of cheap workers minimized the risks of enterprisers and facilitated the adoption of all sorts of innovations and inventions.

There had been analogous developments in Europe. But the Old World had only been able to recruit its proletariat after part of its own population had sunk into pauperism. In America, the laborers were outsiders; industrialization had no adverse effect upon the natives. The whole development came without any constriction in consumer demand such as in Europe followed the fall in purchasing power of the laboring classes; in fact, the rapid growth of numbers actually widened the internal market in the United States and further stimulated industrial and agricultural growth.

The pressure of immigration also made American society fluid enough to keep alive the poor man's dream of a rise in station for himself or for his children. The increase of the population at the lowest economic levels expanded enormously the range of opportunities at every other level. The immigrants themselves were not their own teachers, managers, and doctors. Their presence created the places to which those longer in the country could climb. In 1900 the experience of a century of expansion seemed to demonstrate that any man could go up the ladder as far as his abilities would take him.

The first fifteen years of the new century seemed not to mark any break from the patterns already established. The expansive forces that had brought the country so far, seemed as vigorous as ever, capable of resolving any temporary difficulties the nation might encounter.

The flow of newcomers from across the ocean continued unabated. Indeed the movement showed greater force than before. Cheaper rates of ocean passage allowed still more people to enter the country. The great European powers, by now involved in a headlong naval race, freely subsidized their steamship lines which cut passenger fares to a competitively low level. When the century opened, it was possible to secure decent steerage accommodations for from nine to fifteen dollars.

As earlier, economic displacements accounted for most of the outpouring. The movement out of western and northern Europe continued through these years. But by now the industrial and agricultural transformations had reached deep into the southern and eastern regions of the continent. Increasingly, the immigrants were men who had been born in Italy, Poland, Austria, Russia, Greece, and the Balkans.

The new Americans followed the identical course of eco-

nomic adjustment as had their predecessors. And the consequence of their addition to the labor force was more stimulat-
ing than before, for, in numbers, this wave far outdistanced
the two previous ones. Mounting steadily, the annual total of
entrants rose to a high of 1,285,000 in 1907; and three times in
the next seven years surpassed the million mark. Only the coming of war in 1914 slackened the tide. The conflict in Europe
closed all borders and made ocean travel hazardous. But, even
then, several hundred thousand got through; and what falling
off there was seemed altogether temporary.

By this time Americans had grown accustomed to think of
increase in numbers as characteristic of their whole society.
The total population still climbed: growth of 16,000,000 in a
decade brought it to a height of 92,000,000 in 1910, and when
the war came it was well on the way to the 105,000,000 it
would reach in 1920. The same conclusion emerged from
every industrial, commercial, or agricultural index; in all alike
were read the promise of further expansion without end, while
the momentary shadow of panic in 1907 hardly ruffled the
prevailing optimistic temper of the times.

The ceaseless mobility of the people reflected the faith in
the validity of that promise. That mobility was both spatial
and social. Unwillingness to allow family ties, religious connections, or attachments to a particular place to hold the individual where he was had always been a persistent quality of
life in the United States. The continuing movements to the
west and to the great cities both expressed the readiness to
pull up roots that outsiders had long noted as characteristic of
Americans.

But the capacity to shift about had another connotation; it
took in also the likelihood of rapid changes in social and economic condition. Quick change of fortunes may never have
reached the extremes of acceleration celebrated by Horatio
Alger. But the legend had a substantial basis in fact. The fluidity of life in general, the looseness of all organizational forms,

and the absence in the law of any devices to protect status made it possible for men to move from rags, if not to riches, at least to decent broadcloth in a lifetime.

Mobility in both senses depended upon more than the absence of ties that bound men to their old places. It also rested upon the lack of barriers that prevented them from entering new places. In both the spatial and the social senses, the population with few exceptions could flow where it could make the most of itself, because constant expansiveness created new opportunities, which any individual could hope to grasp. It was the continued existence of those opportunities, as well as the material abundance in which Americans measured their well being, that sustained their confidence in the future. Critics and skeptics indulged their gloom; but these happy years before 1915 were hardly hospitable soil for the seeds of any doubt that the elemental forces of expansion so familiar in the past might cease to be so in the future.

CHAPTER II

The Color Line

American expansiveness made many problems of adjustment easier. People, moving freely where opportunity dictated, occasionally jostled each other, but rarely were provoked to open conflict. There was room for almost everyone. Only at one spot had the development of this society produced a dead area. In that area movement was not free; insurmountable barriers of inequality stood ominously in the way.

The long and tragic history that had divided black from white men had defined that area. In 1900, color drew a line around several million people who were thereby condemned to permanent inferiority of place. Denied the full mobility with which other Americans sought out opportunities, the Negroes could not help but behave as a group apart.

As the new century opened, memories were still fresh of the bitter war of 1861 and of the unhappy peace that followed. But the situation of the black men was not due simply to that painful crisis. It was the outcome of a longer chain of development that went back to the very first settlement of the English colonies in North America.

The Negroes were long since familiar figures on the scene. The time was already out of mind when the first of them had been immigrants to the New World. In the seventeenth century, the earliest to appear had come in the general current of trade that brought to a continent hungry for labor the reluctant masses of Africans and Europeans. All of these newcomers — black and white — toiled under some degree of unfreedom; they were bound servants for greater or lesser terms. But before the century was over, the settlement and acculturation of the Negroes had taken forms that diverged radically from that of other Americans.

In the South, their adjustment had become involved with the plantation. As the large-scale cultivation of tobacco and rice developed after 1680, the black labor force was driven into unmitigated bondage. While the white servants steadily freed themselves of old obligations, the blacks were frozen in their servility. As Americans ceased to think of a society in which many gradations were possible between the free and the unfree, and as they learned to draw a distinct line between liberty and slavery, the Negroes' exceptional servitude grew constantly more onerous.

By the last quarter of the eighteenth century, the most optimistic Southerners, who thought the end of slavery a foreseeable possibility, realized there would be difficulties in leading out of bondage a population brought up in its darkness. But these contemporaries of Jefferson, convinced that all human differences originated in environmental influences, somehow hoped that even the difference in color would ultimately fade out in the beneficent atmosphere of the new republic.

The emergence of cotton culture and the spread of the plantation economy after 1820 abruptly ended that hope. Slavery, strengthened, began to expand rather than to contract. In the southeastern states, Negroes now increased more rapidly in number than whites. The masters of the plantations were apt to encourage the multiplication of the black hands; and the very existence of unfree labor discouraged the immigration of white newcomers, unwilling to compete under the unequal terms of a slave economy.

Indeed, as cotton culture fixed the plantation more firmly into the way of life of the South, it also fixed more rigidly the status of the Negro. The legal terms of his bondage became more stringent, the possibility of emancipation narrower, and the regulation of the emancipated more restrictive. And after 1830, as the abolitionists launched an uncompromising attack upon the whole institution, the defenders of slavery came to justify it as a positive good, worthy of perpetuation and of extension.

The Civil War destroyed slavery, put the old form of servitude altogether outside the law. But emancipation by no means resolved the dilemmas of the Negroes' anomalous position. Two centuries of degradation hardly left the freedmen in a position to take up the responsibilities of citizenship. And their former masters were, from the start, resolved to maintain the old differences. Only three years after the peace, a perceptive Richmond editor pointed to the necessity of erecting new barriers against racial equality. White supremacy might be extended indefinitely, E. A. Pollard explained, by "retaining the Negro as a labourer, and keeping him in a condition where his *political* influence is as indifferent as when he was a slave." [1]

The state governments, reconstituted a few years after Appomattox, immediately began to reforge the caste-like elements of the Negroes' subjection. Black codes made explicit the freedman's social inferiority and reduced him to economic peonage. In some places a brief interlude of reconstruction under radical administrations delayed the trend. But, after 1877, the last of these, discredited, disappeared. Abandoned by the Northern Republicans and helpless before the hostility of both poor whites and former planters, the Southern Negroes entered the dark period of their liberation. By the end of the century, they had been deprived of the suffrage through a variety of subterfuges, they had been excluded from the social life of their communities, and they were depressed by a pervasive pattern of segregation that perpetuated their inferiority.

Yet for neither blacks nor whites was there much comfort

in this solution. If the whites had the advantage of temporary superiority, they had also the anxious fear of losing that advantage. If for the time being they held political and social control, the enjoyment of it was marred by consciousness that the necessary means ran counter to every assumption of American democracy. As for the Negroes themselves, demoralized and discouraged, without effective leadership, they were alternately resentful or resigned, never certain of what goals were attainable in this society.

As the new century opened, Southerners of both races were aware they had reached an impasse. At best, some whites could console themselves that the situation was not growing worse. The rate of Negro increase declined in the last decades of the nineteenth century. The blacks were not now keeping up in growth with the whites. Though there were close to nine million Negroes in the United States in 1900, they were a smaller percentage of the total population than earlier in the century. In 1790 they had been fully 19.3 per cent of the population; by the opening of the twentieth century they were only 11.6 per cent.

For the Negro, the South held only bitter memories and meager prospects. Still it was home; and emancipation did not at once induce him to desert it. The attachment to familiar places and to the known circle of acquaintances held many where they were. Others were immobilized by their own poverty, which deprived them of the means to move elsewhere, which deprived them of the very energy to think of alternatives. Finally, the great majority quickly became entangled in a mesh of debtor and tenant relationships that bound them down as effectively as slavery once had.

Relatively few therefore seriously contemplated flight outside the region. In the 1870's and 1880's some thousands began the migration westward into Arkansas, Texas, Indian Territory, and Kansas, areas into which cotton culture was then spreading. But in these states the newcomers discovered also

the Southern social patterns; the migration rarely effected an
improvement in their condition.

Others moved northward across the Mason-Dixon line to
districts where slavery had withered away before the Civil
War. There the fate of the Negro offered a marked contrast
to his experience in the South.

There had been black men in New England and in the middle states since early colonial times. Always few in numbers,
with no concentrations save in the cities, they had never felt
the rigors of plantation discipline. Adjusting as individuals,
some had already achieved their independence by the middle
of the eighteenth century. Through most of this area, the
Revolution had brought freedom to all.

After 1800, their situation improved steadily, if slowly. As
a group they were often inferior in situation to the majority
of whites. Handicapped by poverty and lack of training, they
found desirable occupational opportunities only with difficulty. Often they made themselves places in the service trades,
held jobs as barbers, waiters, and servants. But some also acquired the skills of artisans and a few penetrated the professions. By the time of the Civil War, they were probably better
off as a group than the recent European immigrants and the
prospect was good of further advances in status.

What hostility the Northern Negroes encountered came
from elements in the population economically more depressed
than they. The white factory workers of the 1860's made the
Negroes occasional butts for resentment; at the depths of the
wartime difficulties, these antagonisms broke out into open
riots. Later, too, rivalry for jobs and for living space bred
jealousies and tensions.

But the favorable elements were stronger still. In the North
the white population grew much more rapidly than the black,
with the Negroes remaining until 1900 only a tiny percentage
of the whole. The humanitarian sentiments stirred up by the
abolitionists had been reinforced with patriotic overtones by

the Civil War and had persisted to the end of the century. Most of all, in the North the colored people were free, where they willed it, to develop an institutional life of their own, a pattern of associations and churches that eased their adjustment in a rapidly expanding society.

To many a downtrodden Southern Negro, therefore, hope seemed to shine only from the North. As the cities grew under the impact of industrialization, as word drifted down of available jobs, a glimmer of expectation appeared in the cabins where only apathy had been before. Now one, or a handful, took the fateful step, broke with the long ties of the familiar and drifted away, daring to exchange the rigidities of home for the opportunities of the distant places. By 1900 there were almost 900,000 above the Mason-Dixon line, with significant little clusters in the largest cities: 67,000 in New York, 64,000 in Philadelphia, 79,000 in Baltimore, 30,150 in Chicago, and 12,000 in Boston.

This foothold in the North was, however, mostly significant for the future. When the twentieth century opened, almost 90 per cent of America's Negroes lived in the South. The conditions of that vast depressed mass set the tone for the status of all.

In the first decades of the new century, the South remained primarily rural; the beginnings of change, in those years, hardly affected the lot of the Negro. The agricultural system had never recovered fully from the destruction of the old plantation economy. Bound to the production of staples — tobacco, cotton, rice, sugar — the soil suffered from erosion and neglect. Those who cultivated it depended at best upon the uncertain returns of fluctuating world markets. But the circumstances under which labor was organized, particularly Negro labor, added to those difficulties further hardships of human creation.

Long before 1900, the freedmen had plunged into a burdensome tenancy relationship from which they still could not escape. Emancipated, they had no land of their own and lacked the cash reserves to take the time to select the means of earning their livelihood. A variety of legal and extralegal pressures drove them back as sharecroppers into the service of their former masters. Compelled each year to borrow for their subsistence against the returns of the next year, they were held in the vise of inescapable obligations that annually left them with no recourse but to take up the same unfavorable contracts.

In the endless round of debts never paid off, there was no incentive for exertion. Stifled, the wild hopes of the freedom time died out. In their place came the demoralized despair of men who took for granted an existence of much labor and few rewards. With no visible purpose to being provident, they lived on in their rickety shacks, consuming what miserable income they earned before ever it was paid to them. The restricted, monotonous diet left them prey to debilitating disease; and lack of amenities, of medical care, and of relief from unremitting toil brought to them a disastrously high death rate.

There were poor whites whose lot was no more enviable, but a heritage of bitter conflict left them rivals rather than allies. Common poverty was not enough to draw the two races together; a tragic past made each seem the cause of the other's misery. The white accounted for his degradation by the presence of the blacks whose competition reduced the return from his own labor. The blacks did indeed show a willingness to accept minimal terms, because only thus could they overcome the preference of the landlord for white tenants or employees. In practice, the masters of the soil used the accumulated fears and hatreds of generations to hold the two groups apart.

The identical division extended into the new activities that marked the region's industrial awakening. In the coal mines, on the railroads, on the docks, employers accepted the docile cheap labor of the Negro who was docile and cheap because he knew he would be taken on only if he accepted terms the whites would not tolerate. A strike or the threat of a strike increased the willingness of hirers to employ black hands; and the hands themselves yielded readily to the tempting access of skilled occupations ordinarily closed to them. But the price of such opportunism was the deep enmity of the white workers who saw in this marginal labor force an insuperable obstacle to the improvement of their own status.

These underlying economic conflicts together with persistent racial antagonism brought to nought tentative steps in the 1890's that might otherwise have led to some measure of coöperation. In that decade, Southern reformers, aflame with Populist grievances against big business, often conceived of their program in terms wide enough to benefit the Negro, indeed sometimes hoped to use the black vote to attain their goals. But the radicals discovered that their political opponents were more capable of turning the ballots of the Negroes to account, just as the early unions had discovered employers able to exploit Negro labor. The injured agrarian and labor reformers increasingly focused their hostility upon the vulnerable Negro rather than upon the powerful planters and industrialists whose instrument he was.

Yet the Negro was trapped. Whatever abstract line of logic should have led him to an alliance with the reformers, his immediate interest lay in coöperation with the conservatives. In practice, he preferred to go along with the bosses who supplied him with a livelihood and upheld law and order of a sort, rather than to take the risks of depending upon those very whites with whom he competed desperately for jobs and for living space. By the opening of the twentieth century, disillusioned Populists had moved to the forefront of the movement to restrict even further the rights of the Negroes.

Now the Negroes were everywhere closed in by unsurmountable barriers of segregation; everywhere they were marked by the indelible signs of their racial inferiority. The pattern of social exclusion was complete. Barred from every institution in which contact with whites might create the imputation of equality, they were taught by the inflexible Jim Crow pattern to accept a complex etiquette of behavior and of relationships through which they demonstrated their subjection to the master race. Laws against intermarriage, against contact in public places and in transportation, codified and perpetuated that pattern. The brief period of alliance with the Southern reformers was over, the former Populists were now their bitterest enemies, and the last vestiges of the Negroes' political rights disappeared. Steadily the suffrage slipped out of the hands of the colored men. Between 1890 and 1909 in each of the old Confederate states, some subterfuge or other made a mockery of the fifteenth amendment. At the end of those decades the poll tax had reappeared throughout the region to "disfranchise the darkies and educate white children." [2] Without access to the power of government, incapable of serving on juries, the blacks were exposed to the unrestrained violence of those who oppressed them. Every year a hundred lynchings reminded any Negro who might have the temerity to think of it, what would be the consequence of resisting white authority. When the riot flared in Atlanta in 1906, the scores of dead were the evidence — not to be questioned — of the force always present and always available to repress any challenge to the propriety of the kind of world that had been made for the colored men.

Steadily the Negroes were driven to accept the white view of that world and of their own place in it. For the great mass there was no practical alternative. At Tuskegee Institute in Alabama, for almost twenty years Booker T. Washington had been pointing the way toward a kind of adjustment. Advising a withdrawal from politics and the surrender of the notion of social equality as an immediate goal, Washington counseled the people of his race to make themselves a tolerable place in the Southern economy. "The opportunity to earn a dollar in a factory just now is worth infinitely more than the opportunity to spend a dollar in an opera house." The Negroes were to direct their energies toward improvement of their vocational status. For the time being, they were to accept the expedient of segregation from the whites, remain "separate as fingers yet one as the hand," in the hope that gradual advance into the middle class would earn the respect of the dominant majority and eventually result in some amelioration of conditions.[3]

For the Negroes who acquired skills and lifted themselves out of the lowest occupations, Washington's teachings explained the limits of their success. It was true society rewarded the virtue and hard work of other Americans with worldly goods and social recognition and withheld those rewards from the blacks; but there was compensation in remembering the distance they had come since slavery and in anticipating the progress yet to follow.

For the mass of colored folk who never advanced beyond the humblest stations, Washington's ideas had a less direct but nonetheless cogent meaning. The counsel of acquiescence supplied an emotional outlet for present sufferings and enabled men to yield, with a modicum of self-respect, to pressures they could not in any case resist. Patience and endurance became the cardinal virtues as well as the only practical mode of behavior. Perhaps Washington found the receptive audience he did because his message supplied a rational equivalent for the kind of consolation his people were accustomed to draw from religion.

Washington rendered plausible to the great mass of Southern Negroes their role in a world that other people made and that they could only slightly control. Although he argued that the fate of the blacks rested in their own hands, he also accepted the assumption that the conditions of their existence would be fixed within limits set by white society. They had freedom to be either good or bad, so long as they understood it was the whites who defined what good or bad behavior was.

The dominant race in the South no longer conceived of a
return to ante-bellum conditions as the ideal. While the literature of the section still put a romantic halo about the old
plantation life, there was in practice no inclination to revert
to the fancied intimacy of personal relationships that had
characterized the old order. Instead the Negro was considered
an incubus, if an indispensable one. His labor was necessary,
for want of any alternative. In fact it was a public duty to
keep him where he was, to prevent him from drifting away to
"the filthy garrets and sickly cellars" of the cities. But the
separateness and inferiority of his place was decisively to be
recognized. The whites now showed little desire to restore
the closeness of the prewar way of life; rather they desired
segregation complete enough to enable the two groups to exist
with a minimum of contact wherever the Negro labor was
needed. Such a planter as Alfred H. Stone, therefore, was willing to accept the appearance of a Negro professional and business class to lessen the occasions for dealings between blacks
and whites. Such tolerance did not run counter to the basic
assumption of ineradicable racial differences. Indeed it gave
that assumption new and more penetrating force. "The purity
and progress of both races" would always "require that caste
. . . be maintained" and that the superior act as guardians and
governors of the inferior.[4]

The hardening patterns of segregation killed off the surviving remnants of humanitarian activity within which Negroes
and whites were treated as equals. In the years after the Civil
War, it was not only the carpetbaggers who had invaded the
South; into the war-torn states there moved also devoted men
and women imbued with the abolitionist outlook and determined to put into practice their ideals of equality. Swayed by
religious zeal they set up schools, colleges, and other institutions open to the two races. These symbols of an earlier optimism flickered on to the close of the century. But they
could not long withstand the stifling force of the new racialist

pressures. The pioneers, dying out, found no successors; and the atmosphere of hostility brought these hopeful experiments to a close. The Berea College Case in 1908 upheld a Kentucky law that forbade schools to teach more than one race and dealt a death blow to all these activities.

With such the white outlook, there was no alternative for the Southern Negro but to adopt the Booker T. Washington philosophy. For those who edged into the professions or who built themselves a competence as businessmen there was some satisfaction in their own relative well-being and in the group leadership their status gave them. Others found rewards for the acquisition of skill in places in industry, the railroads, or the mines. But all these remained the minority. And the minority itself knew always it managed to get along only through the indulgence of the whites. Too much progress brought the risk of reprisal from those edged out, or who thought that they might be edged out. Direct violence sometimes met the intruding black man; or sometimes, it was a strike as in the railways which set up quotas, wage differentials, or some other limits beyond which he could not advance. Not many under these conditions lived by any code but resignation.

Therefore it was still to the North that those who wished a larger freedom looked. Again and again the word passed south of opportunities available in the more fluid society above the Mason-Dixon line — from Negroes already established there, through the press, or from employers on the lookout for cheap or strike-breaking labor. The number who actually took the road away from home was small in comparison with those who remained. But the migration steadily built up the size of the communities in the great cities of the North; by 1910 there were more than ninety thousand colored folk in New York, eighty-four thousand in Philadelphia, and forty-four thousand in Chicago.

However, the brutal fact was that the position of the Negro masses was deteriorating in the North too. There was not here the harsh pattern of segregation. There were opportunities for schooling that led those lucky enough to make use of it into the professions. Yet the newcomer from the South discovered he was entering a market plentifully stocked with immigrant labor, a market in which there was little demand for his services. In the welter of competition for places in industry, not many found the means of raising themselves.

Indeed, even the Negroes long settled in the North viewed the future with some trepidation. In part their fears were occasioned by the immigration of others of their race. The influx cramped the available residential areas. The poor and ignorant newcomers, rustic in habits and demeanor, lowered the status of all identified with them. The long-established Negroes at first recoiled from the primitive newcomers, but nevertheless found that color, in the eyes of the whites, made all blacks one. At the same time all but the most secure faced a genuine threat to their old hold on the service occupations; cheap white immigrant labor now competed for kinds of jobs formerly exclusively theirs, as Italians, Greeks, and others became barbers, shoe shine boys, waiters, and domestics. Finally the growing prevalence of racialist ideas throughout the United States made the Negro's situation everywhere less tenable.

The difficulties of urban living lent new complexity to the problems of the race. To the Negroes capable of reading the meaning of these events and to the philanthropic whites concerned with their lot, it was clear that amelioration within the existing order of things called for determined positive measures. In the first decade of the new century, a cluster of societies set themselves the task of widening the opportunities for Negro employment. In 1911, a number of these associations united their efforts in the National Urban League, which thereafter was in the forefront of this struggle.

The mass of Negroes, North and South, were however hardly aware of the zealous activity on their behalf by social workers and reformers. Surely any one among the black men would have welcomed the opportunities for which the League strove; but its objectives scarcely seemed real. Deprived by their situation of the luxurious certitude of progress that other Americans took for granted, the Negroes devoted the largest part of their energies to the immediate difficulties of survival. What time and attention and energy were left, they gave over to an active religious life that promised, at least, consolation.

The churches were central to Negro communal life. Since the first organization of Negro churches at the end of the eighteenth century, these had developed rapidly, at first in the Northern cities, then spreading southward after emancipation.

To a large measure these associations were voluntary. Historically, their inception had been a token of the colored people's assertiveness of their own social self-confidence and that quality, inherited from the very origins of these churches, still clung to them in 1900. Of course the white churches, when they admitted Negroes at all, generally confined them to an inferior status. But it was more than that that drove the Negro to institute churches of his own; he wished to be more than a passive listener, wished for a form of religion in which he could express in his own way, his own view of his God and his world. Those ends he was not as likely to attain among the whites, whom the social import of color made strangers, as within the communion of his own kind.

Sooner or later, there were independent Negro churches within, or affiliated with, or parallel to almost every branch of American Christianity. But the spontaneous generation of these churches, and the fact that often they depended for long periods on lay preachers, made it easiest to organize such congregations in the evangelical denominations and particularly among the Methodists and Baptists. The inclination of the mass of members toward an emotional and demonstrative religion increased the attractiveness of these forms of Protestantism.

No rigid denominational affiliation however contained all the inchoate strivings of the group. As the churches multiplied in number, they also multiplied in factions. Rapid growth testified to the intimacy of the hold upon their members; each worshipper insisted that the church be uniquely his, responsive to his inexpressible yearnings, rather than constricted within some formal creed. In some places the churches constructed respectable buildings, in others they took over the edifices abandoned by whites; and still elsewhere they served their communicants in humble stores. In all, by 1906 the number of congregations had grown to about 40,000, of which 35,000 had buildings of their own. The development had been particularly impressive in the years after 1890.

The urge for fellowship that drew Negroes together in prayer also drew them together for other modes of communal action as they confronted the major contingencies of life as free but powerless men. Detached and insecure, the individual was altogether incapable of coping with the hazards of living and dying. The funeral would not wait upon a man's ability to pay for it, nor illness; and alone it was difficult to prepare against the inevitable needs. Like the members of the Grand United Order of Moses, many a Negro felt it well to have an organization that would help the poor, furnish benefits against sickness, accident, and death, and, at the same time, "unite the people in principles of religion, intelligence, morality, temperance, and character" and help their children obtain a "practical higher education." [5]

In addition to the insurance functions, the mutual-aid organizations, through ritual and through elaborate patterns of social activity, also supplied their members with a sense of belonging, allowed some to play the role of leaders, and gave all the consciousness of common purpose. Yet, though these associations served everywhere the same ends, there was no uniformity in the means by which they did so. Their character depended upon local conditions and upon the needs of those who participated in them. The society might be connected with a church or not, it might be part of some national order like the Elks or altogether the product of a handful of members, it might, like the Masons, have a history that reached back to the eighteenth century, or it might have come only recently into existence. The society was what its members made it.

The Negro found another means of expression in the press. None of the old abolitionist newspapers had survived the Civil War. But the 1880's saw the appearance of a newer, more vigorous type. Young men with some experience in journalism, occasionally, as in the case of C. J. Perry, with experience on the "Colored Department" of a metropolitan publication, established a succession of weeklies still small in circulation but growing in influence. These editors were interested in their enterprises as businesses, but they were also concerned with the defense of the rights of colored men. Frequently, however, the publishers who were often also G.O.P. officeholders identified those rights with the fate of the Republican Party, and used their papers to mobilize the Negro vote. But the primary function of these newspapers was to provide the supplementary information of the affairs of the Negro communities in the United States that did not find their way into the more general press. Eagerness for such news after 1880 created the reading public for the *Richmond Planet*, the *Cleveland Gazette*, the *Philadelphia Tribune*, and the *New York Age*. These papers were joined after 1890 by the *Afro-American*, and after 1900 by the *Norfolk Journal*, the *Chicago Defender*, the *Amsterdam News*, and the *Pittsburgh Courier*. In addition a host of denominational and fraternal journals brought the total to some four hundred by 1914.

No doubt, a continuing consciousness of the barriers that

color could raise subtly influenced colored people as they became involved in these activities. But the attractive power of the churches, the fraternal orders, and the press sprang from the awareness by the Negroes of their separateness as a group in American society and from their desire to lead a life of their own. The vitality and variety of these social organizations and the fact that control continued to rest in the hands of colored people testified to the genuinely voluntary quality of such affiliations.

It was otherwise in activities within which the Negro was not free to set the terms of his own participation. Education for instance was a matter of public concern, controlled by the state, and supported by taxes. The dominant whites determined by law to what extent the black man would have schools of his own and also what the nature of those institutions would be.

In the South, by 1900 the pattern of segregated education was almost complete. Negroes there would have what training they could get in separate schools, which nevertheless were not their own. Subsisting on the minimal remnants of public funds that could be spared for them and generally directed by whites, these never provided adequate training and certainly did not become vital parts of the life of the Negro group.

Even the institutions of higher learning, though established by men interested in the welfare of the former slaves, suffered from the liability that they were controlled by outsiders and were unresponsive to the needs of those they attempted to serve. Tuskegee, within its limited objectives, was more successful. Its simple, vocational ends were more meaningful in terms of the situation of the mass of Negroes; and it was their own. That in part explained the peculiar attachment of its people to it.

Although in most sections of the North the ideal of free, equal, and undiscriminating education persisted, the ideal was considerably diluted by patterns of discrimination tolerated by law. Pennsylvania, for instance, openly permitted communities to establish separate schools, or where that was financially difficult, to set aside "Union Rooms" into which Negro children were herded without regard to grade. Elsewhere residential concentration drew colored students off into elementary schools largely their own. Few anywhere had the background or the means of advancing on to a higher education and those that did often found the way to college barred by informal measures of discrimination. As a result it was not unusual for Northern Negroes to go south for advanced studies.

The few who did break through into the classrooms of Harvard or Columbia or Oberlin got a more adequate training than was anywhere else available. It was significant that the leadership for the next generation of Negroes would come from graduates of these institutions rather than from the segregated colleges and universities. But the stark fact was that, North and South, what education the Negro got depended not in the least upon his own choice. In that respect the arrangements made for him conformed to the more general Jim Crow patterns. Every colored child, who had not already learned it at home, discovered as he entered the school that other people's judgments, based on his color, would always limit the kinds of activity in which he would be free to engage.

For the mass of Negroes, the dilemmas involved were only slightly oppressive; they lived and labored with the closed rounds of harsh tasks within which they might vaguely sense, but could hardly define, the freedoms they lacked. But the burden was cruel for those who succeeded in improving their economic, professional, or intellectual situation and were nevertheless prevented by their color from moving to the levels of society their attainments justified. Now and then it was possible for one favored by the accidents of pigmentation to pass surreptitiously outside the narrow confines set by the prevailing race conceptions. But such passing involved an inner conflict; it was infrequent; and it depended upon the whims of nature rather than the plans of man. Most Negroes found the ordinary channels of American mobility closed to them.

Those with a foothold in business or the professions were sometimes tempted to establish a distance between themselves and the mass of Negroes who seemed to drag them down. Those advanced in culture and in wealth longed to have their due in social recognition and yielded often to the hope they might earn it by conforming to the standards of other, more fortunate Americans. Perhaps good manners and proper clothing or genteel speech would turn away the adverse criticisms and open the way to social acceptance. A progressive movement in religion aspired to make the colored churches more like those of the whites, to substitute an organ for congregational singing, to displace the emotional lay preachers, to introduce a greater sense of decorum. The inevitable outcome was the fashionable Negro parish with serious pretensions to social superiority.

Negroes with such aspirations also learned much by observing the techniques of white exclusiveness. They formed literary, charitable, and social clubs with select memberships, often with genealogical or geographical qualifications, to mark off the colored people of quality. Insofar as it was possible the well-to-do Negroes also attempted to set themselves off in more desirable residential districts and to provide themselves with dignified places of entertainment closed to the mass with whom white society associated them. Although rejected by that larger society, they yet established a Negro aristocracy based on proximity to white standards, to some extent actually on proximity to white coloring.

Upper-class Negroes lived, therefore, under the uneasy strain of avoiding wounds to their self-esteem; the racial slight, reminder of their identity with all those who were once slaves, hung always over their heads. Safety lay in the sedulous evasion of racial issues and in the patient struggle to endow their own existences with order and stability.

Yet it was stability they lacked most of all. These people had rarely the opportunity to accumulate family holdings of capital or land; they were, after all, rich only by comparison with other Negroes. Indeed this aristocracy could never establish the permanent attributes of class status. It was consequently easily penetrated after 1900 by professional men — ministers, journalists, lawyers, physicians, and teachers — men whose credentials were not those of inherited or earned fortunes but of educational qualifications respected in the white world and economically useful in the black. Breaking quickly through to positions of leadership in the Negro upper class, a relatively small group of intellectuals acquired far-reaching influence.

Intellectuals, particularly Northern intellectuals, found Booker T. Washington's solution utterly irrelevant. The advice to acquire skills was altogther supererogatory while the immediate compromises with self-respect were painfully intolerable; for to these Negroes, brought up to believe in the American promises of equality and progress, the dim prospect of some compensating eventual acceptance by the whites was worth little.

The rebuffs by a white society that refused to acknowledge their attainments came as a shock to these men. Not a few turned their backs upon the white standards which had seemed to play them false. Unable to be entire Americans they sought to be entire Negroes and created from their frustrations the image of a group with which they could completely identify themselves. "A new loyalty and allegiance replaced my Americanism," wrote one of them at the time when he entered Fisk, "henceforward I was a Negro." [6]

Even as they uttered the ringing statements, these people

were not clear as to what their Negro identification meant. Thinking in terms of the American scene in which culture was most often defined in terms of some overseas antecedent, the colored intellectuals were inclined to look back to their African origins. They often explained themselves as Afro-Americans, just as others among their contemporaries referred to themselves as Irish-Americans or German-Americans.

A drastic transformation of attitudes followed this new awareness of their own identity. Thus, W. E. B. DuBois, raised in Great Barrington, Massachusetts, and holder of a doctorate from Harvard, in *The Souls of Black Folk* (1903), not only expressed his sense of unity with all blacks, but at the same time called for a rejection of Booker T. Washington's outlook. Ultimately, DuBois thought, the Negro would express himself in his own way in every cultural medium; but his minimal obligation was at once to fight in defense of his own immediate rights. There could be no tolerable apology for injustice, and the Negro could accept nothing less than equality. DuBois openly pronounced the whites the enemies of his people and called for the training of a Negro leadership to conduct the battle against prejudice.

But it was painfully difficult to make a reality of the aspiration. Back in 1890, J. C. Price and T. T. Fortune had issued a call for an Afro-American Council. Their appeal fell upon deaf ears. The same fate met the summons of the militant *Boston Guardian* in 1901. An excited conference at Niagara Falls in 1905 and the fervid pilgrimage to Harpers Ferry a year later were tokens of the Negroes' obdurate consciousness of their identity, but had no continuing effect.

The intellectuals involved in these efforts had laid down a clear intellectual line. But they had not the resources or the mass support to transform that line into an organized movement. In the main, colored Americans still felt bound to the day-to-day pattern of compromise and mediation and acquiescence.

The decisive step in the struggle for equal rights was therefore not one that recognized any particular Negro stake in
the issue or that allowed him any autonomous role in its resolution. The battle proceeded instead from the premise that
the problems of race were those of the whole society; and the
positions of command in that battle were generally in the
hands of whites.

The bloody riots in Springfield, Illinois, in 1908 had
shocked many men still moved by humanitarian sentiments
inherited from the abolition movement. W. E. Walling, O. G.
Villard, and Moorfield Storey, among others, were dismayed
at the realization that prejudice could take such an overt,
violent form in a Northern state, indeed in the home of the
Great Emancipator. Their dismay led to the foundation of
the National Association for the Advancement of Colored
People in 1910.

Markedly influenced in the formulation of its platform by
the protests of such Negroes as DuBois, the N.A.A.C.P.
called for equality of civil and legal rights and for complete
access to education and to the franchise. It thus rejected the
compromises of Booker T. Washington. But it also rejected
DuBois's assumption of the oneness of the Negroes, of their
separateness from the whites. Like the organizations which
a year later combined into the National Urban League, the
N.A.A.C.P. held that the issues involved interested not the
Negroes exclusively, but all Americans.

Intransigent Negroes like W. M. Trotter, therefore, holding to the dogma that there could be no collaboration in the
struggle, remained aloof. But DuBois's reaction was more
typical. He had turned his back upon his white connections to
go to Atlanta, Georgia, confident that in the combined role
of teacher, scholar, and social worker he would demonstrate
the capacity of an elite to raise the level of the whole Negro
community. Cruel frustrations had eaten away that confidence. Although his personal emotional attachment to the

conception of the identity of the Negro group remained as strong as ever, the practical necessities compelled him to accept a program of action intrinsically contradictory. He threw in his lot with the N.A.A.C.P.

But then, such contradictions were implicit in the situation of the Negroes in the United States. Color had put a bar across the society that took for granted the mobility of the individual in an expanding culture. Black Americans, prevented from making free personal adjustments as wage earners or citizens, accepted perforce a pattern of accommodation and compromise that prevented them also from developing a group life on their own terms. In every area in which their actions touched upon the interests of the whites, it was the whites who determined whether the Negroes were to stand apart or not. That would be a continuing source of dilemmas.

The history of the Negroes in the United States had imparted a blight to the idea of color, so that Americans in the twentieth century found it difficult to deal with any man without taking account of differences of skin pigmentation. But the whites had, at the end of the nineteenth century, no fixed conception of any absolute standard of color. Even in their relationships to Negroes they were accustomed to variations that ranged from the pale octoroon to the full-blooded black. It was not any defined shade of darkness that made such people Negroes, but rather the fact that they were Negroes that cast an odium on their color.

Americans had long had other contacts with other people who were not white under circumstances which attached no particular stigma to color. The indigenous Indians, the Chinese, the South Sea Islanders, the Hindus, encountered as images in literature or as real characters in the course of westward expansion, trade, or missionary activity aroused no sense of antipathy or even of inherent racial difference. Through most of the nineteenth century, the prevailing

American conception of human equality ascribed differences in skin color simply to the effect of differences of environment. Except for the Negro!

But it was not long possible to seal off the attitudes toward the blacks as exceptional. The continuing prominence of the problems of the former slaves pushed to the fore the question as to the significance of their pigmentation. Racialist ideas, developed to justify the inferiority of the Negro, raised troubling implications for the status of all men who were not white.

In time, people from all corners of the globe appeared in the United States, often under conditions reminiscent of those of the Negro; their presence was a challenge toward definition of the meaning of color. Often at last, some specific issue precipitated a conflict in the course of which the dominant Americans transferred to one group after another, alike in no other respect, the attitudes developed toward the Negro. The conception of color thus expanded to take in a variety of peoples who had in common only the inferiority of relationships imposed on them by those who defined themselves as whites.

By 1900 this had already been the experience of the Chinese. Once, indeed, Californians had regarded these immigrants with favor, welcomed their labor, and looked with hope to their quick assimilation into the life of the Pacific coast. But a decisive reversal of opinions after 1870 closed all doors against them. For thirty years thereafter a succession of turbulent movements had agitated against the very presence of these people in the United States. Frequent outbreaks of violence had threatened them, and a series of discriminatory local laws had put them in a completely separate category. The courts had barred them from citizenship and congressional legislation in 1882, 1888, and 1892 had suspended all substantial immigration of Chinese.

A few no doubt entered the country illegally, by ship or

over the Canadian or Mexican borders. But with no appreci-
able additions, with a low birth rate that was the product of
urbanization and the preponderance of males, the group
shrank in size. Over 107,000 in 1890, the Chinese counted
less than 90,000 in 1900, and were to fall to some 70,000 in
1910. By the opening of the twentieth century they had concentrated in the urban centers of the West coast and in a few
large eastern cities. They were by then economically stable
and well adjusted. A few were employed in the cigar and
clothing industries. But mostly they labored in laundries, in
restaurants, or in the service occupations where they competed with no one. Their communal life was active and
adequate. They still lived in slums at the low standard that
was the result of low earning powers. Yet the fears earlier
associated with these mysterious districts had largely vanished.
It was clear that their benevolent societies, the tongs, were
not the sinister bodies feverish imaginations had once made
them but rather mutual assistance organizations that maintained cemeteries, settled disputes among members, extended
charity, and kept the Chinese from being a burden to any
one. In addition, district and family societies helped fight the
pangs of loneliness and afternoon schools taught children the
ancestral language. The press and political organizations such
as the Chinese-American Citizens Alliance, or the Chinese
Free Masons' Association were interested both in assisting
the Chinese to adjust to their life in America and in further-
ing programs of reform and constitutionalism in the Celestial
Empire itself.

But this tiny group was not allowed to sink out of public
notice. Identified as colored by Southerners who brought to
California not only Negro servants but also confirmed habits
of thought about race, or conflated by the frontiersmen with
the Diggers and other low, barbarous Indians, the Chinese
encountered a mounting current of prejudice that any element
interested in doing so could exploit. Hostile agitation con-

tinued on the Pacific coast and the organized labor movement spread hatred of the Chinese to every part of the nation. In 1901, Samuel Gompers in *Bread v. Rice*, set forth the thesis that the civilizations of the brown men and the white could never accommodate themselves; and that year the American Federation of Labor devoted a good part of its annual convention to discussion of the means to fight the peril of further Chinese immigration. In 1902, the law made their exclusion permanent; and those already in the United States were denied the right of naturalization, a right already in practice withheld by the courts.

Whatever potential threat there may have been in the remote possibility that Chinese immigration would be resumed was certainly not imminent enough to stir the labor leaders into the frenzied action they took. Behind these immediate acts was a cumulated heritage of prejudice made more sensitive when a new empire in the Philippines and the Caribbean added to the United States millions of colored inhabitants, described as inferior by the propaganda of the imperialists.

The force of these prejudices speedily extended their effects to other groups which were not open to the specific charges levelled against the Chinese. The residents of the Celestial Empire had been attacked as slothful, deceitful, unwilling to conform to American ways, and dulled to a low standard of living; other folk were attacked because they were aggressive, good business people, and too readily aped American ways and living standards.

The Japanese had only recently arrived; until 1885 the Mikado's government prohibited emigration. By the end of the century only twelve thousand of his subjects had reached the United States. These newcomers benefited at first from the romantic conceptions Americans since Perry's day had held of the island of flowers and kimonas. The accounts of Lafcadio Hearn and of Percival Lowell, which emphasized the picturesque qualities of their differences, strengthened that attitude as did Theodore Roosevelt's foreign policy which anticipated a working collaboration in the exploitation of the Far East. The aura of sentimental approval emerged from the treatment of the Japanese in John L. Long's *Madame Butterfly*. When the war against Russia came a few years later, most Americans still sympathized with the gentle little men who gallantly resisted the mammoth Czarist empire.

If the favorable attitude changed in the first decade of the twentieth century, it was not because of any undesirable attributes in the Japanese immigration after 1900. The volume was low — only a little over ninety thousand between 1901 and 1910 — and the adjustment of the newcomers was satisfactory. They filled a useful role in agriculture, worked hard, thrived, sent their children to the public schools, and met and solved the usual problems of adaptation to a new environment. But already there were signs of trepidation along the Pacific coast and within the labor movement, although these were of little consequence until 1905.

In 1905 and 1906 a series of discontinuous events suddenly focused the fear of color upon the Japanese with explosive consequences. A newspaper publisher with political ambitions sponsored a series of widely read articles on the menace of the Nipponese invaders. A group of nativists organized to secure the exclusion of the brown men. And a San Francisco political gang, on the verge of exposure, dragged out the racial issue to divert attention from itself. Mayor Schmitz and Boss Ruef who ordered the Japanese children of San Francisco into segregated schools were not seriously worried over the disposition of the ninety-three youngsters involved. They acted rather from the simple desire to stir up enough confusion among the city's voters to obscure the unpleasant findings of a grand jury then investigating the municipal administration. But the immediate repercussions were evidence of the stored up prejudice into which their spark fell. Anti-Japanese sentiment spread like wildfire along the coast and then eastward. Editorials in cities where few Japanese had ever been seen nevertheless concluded those people would never become Americans. "They are clean, well mannered, and industrious; better folk by far . . . than a good many other newcomers. But they are not our kind, and will not merge." In a matter of weeks a vociferous call for exclusion reached Washington.[7]

This turn of affairs seriously embarrassed President Roosevelt, anxious to maintain good relationships with Tokyo. In the effort to save everyone's face, the Gentlemen's Agreement of 1907 gave the exclusionists what they wished without the necessity of a formal act of Congress. By the understanding, Japan undertook to prevent the emigration of its subjects of the laboring class. Still, even that concession did not long maintain stability. Six years later the California legislature enacted a grossly discriminatory law that prevented Japanese from owning land in the state, and no amount of reassurance would quiet the suspicion that the Nipponese were evading their obligations.

Upon the Japanese firmly settled in the United States, the course of this agitation had a profound effect. They had created a wide range of organizations to assist their adjustment to the life of their new country. Through prefectural clubs, newspapers, labor unions, producers' associations, and a variety of mutual aid societies they had dealt with the variety of problems that all newcomers encountered. They had also wished to hold to the old language and the old religion, setting up afternoon Japanese schools for their children and building Buddhist shrines for worship. But "an American Buddhist plant with its gymnasium, library, auditorium, and various rooms for educational and social purposes" bore little resemblance to the temples of the Old World; it represented rather the beginnings of conformity to American conditions.[8]

Precisely because the Japanese had been so anxious to conform to American ways, rejection by the society around them came as a profound shock. The pressures from without turned their loyalties inward. Having no one else to rely upon, they were more closely tied than ever to their own organizations for mutual aid. Indeed they were sometimes tempted to look to Tokyo for guidance and were inclined to rely upon the Japanese Association, a body controlled by its American members, but nevertheless, in some ways, an arm of the Japanese government. The Gentlemen's Agreement inadvertently strengthened the hold of the Association. Since regulation of any further immigration rested in Tokyo, Japanese-Americans who wished to secure admission of members of their families or of brides naturally turned to the Association to secure the necessary consent.

A handful of Hindus who had wandered to the Pacific coast were greeted with similar race hostility of a virulence altogether disproportionate to their numbers which never rose above six thousand. Coming in the first decades of the new century, mostly Sikhs from the Punjab, these people had worked as migrant laborers in the rice lands of the Sacramento Valley, in the cotton lands of the Imperial Valley, and in the lumber mills of Oregon. Few in number, they developed a communal life only slowly. A handful of temples and the Khalsa Divan, a mutual aid society, were the extent of their organization in the United States. Yet their exotic appearance had at once earned them the designation "ragheads"; and fear of their color precipitated riots in Bellingham, Washington, in Live Oak, California, and in Saint John, Oregon, between 1907 and 1910.

The Chinese, Japanese, and Hindus had little in common other than their situation in America. In the course of the developing hostility against them, they acquired the odium as people of color already attached to the Negro. Although there were grounds for considering them "white" within the meaning of the Constitution, the courts held them ineligible for citizenship and, as in the case of the blacks, extended the taint of color even to the children of mixed marriages. The bitterness of the prejudices by then involved emerged from the complaint of a California farmer, "Near my home . . . lives a Japanese. With that Japanese lives a white woman. In that woman's arms is a baby. . . . That baby . . . is a germ of the mightiest problem that ever faced this state; a problem that will make the black problem of the South look white." [9]

But though these people were quickly identified as colored, there was uncertainty about just what their color was. The first attacks on the Chinese were against the little brown rice-eaters. The addition of the Japanese created some complexities for those who sought a common denominator of color. The specter of the Yellow Peril ended the indecision; thereafter the Oriental or Asiatic was the Yellow Man.

Yet although color itself was now divisive enough to set Negroes and Orientals off from the white Americans, there were still ambiguities in the conception of color itself. The stigmata originally attached to the Negro's symbol of his servile antecedents had spread to other, dissimilar, people. But how far could Americans go in defining the shades of non-white skin pigmentation as colored? If any offspring of a mixed marriage, no matter how light, was colored, was there any external standard criterion by which the judgment could be made? Other groups, neither Negro nor Oriental, would await the test of American scrutiny before they knew whether they belonged on one side or the other of the color line.

The acquisition of the Spanish colonies had brought under the American flag a host of people who raised that problem. Scattered individuals from the Philippines, from Cuba, from Puerto Rico, and from Hawaii were already making their way to the United States; and others would follow in growing numbers. Nor would that be the limit. Syrians and Turks and Arabs and Armenians would in time pose the question of what was an Asiatic or Oriental; and Mexicans and Italians, the question of how dark it was possible to be without ceasing to be white. With regard to some of these issues the courts had already passed preliminary judgment; but experience had shown that judges were capable of reversing themselves in such matters.

The color line would have been perplexing enough even had no newcomers complicated it. The American Indian was certainly native to the soil. But, with the shade of a man's skin so critically important, Americans began to wonder where the Indian fitted.

The compilers of the federal census had their own opinion. In their statistics, they joined together Indians and Mongolian Asiatics. Similarly, in cases involving the naturalization of Canadian and South American Indians, the judges ruled the red men no more eligible than the yellow. But that classification was not everywhere recognized. Though there were regions in the Southwest where the Indian was reckoned an inferior like other colored men, the more general assumption was that he would gradually, if slowly, approach the white in culture and ultimately lose his identity in intermarriage.

The nineteenth-century Indian had suffered from the hostility of advancing settlers who feared his attack and who coveted his land. But with the close of the frontier and the disappearance of the red men's organized power, that source of antagonism became less important.

By the end of the century, Indians were expected in due course to enter white society and to fuse with those who had replaced them on the land. That expectation was fed by the old romantic ideas of the Indian as the noble savage endowed with primitive virtue; it was supported by scientific arguments drawn from the theories of evolution and the survival of the fittest; and it was motivated by humanitarian regrets at injustices once done the aborigines. Furthermore, events seemed to prove the soundness of the notion the Indians would soon vanish as a group. Their numbers declined to a low point of about a quarter million shortly after the turn of the century. A steady stream of whites and Negroes, attracted by the rights of the red men to tribal lands, married into the group, while the enticements of the world outside the reservation drew away a return flow of former tribesmen.

The assumption that the Indians would lose their identity in the society around them was written into government policy by the Dawes Act (1887) which provided for the liquidation of tribal property held in common in favor of individual allotments. "The enjoyment and pride of individual ownership of property," it was reasoned, was "one of the most effective civilizing agencies." [10] Well-intentioned as it was, that law created serious difficulties for the Indians. In practice it was hard to make the transition, to enter the white society in a dignified manner; and a good deal of the land found its way into the hands of white owners.

It was also hard to fit the old tribal institutions to the new conditions. There was a great variety of conditions among the Indians, from the prosperous landowner and husbandman to the shiftless day laborer. But among all there was a sense they had not been able to "evolve a sort of civilization that would suit our temperament." [11] Although they began to increase in numbers after 1905, the red men were hardly content. For their communal life labored under the strain of the assumption that it would disappear. If these people were not to be counted colored, with all the disabilities that designation involved, then they were expected to become whites. That demand seemed to leave no focus for a meaningful group life. Communal integrity was sacrificed, as it were, to the necessity of finding a place on one side or the other of the color line.

That line in the opening decade of the twentieth century in a variety of forms had separated substantial groups of people from the rest of the population. By limiting the voluntary adjustments and circumscribing the kinds of choices available to Negroes, Orientals, and Indians, it had cast in a rigid mold activities that remained spontaneous and fluid for others. It thus set aside groups that did not share fully in the mobility and expansiveness of American society.

CHAPTER III

The Migrations

The arbitrary quality of the color line obscured the more important diversities on either side of it. The whites were united only insofar as the line made them so; in the most important aspects of their social life, they fell into a variety of groups which differed widely from one another.

Those groups, by contrast to the Negroes and Orientals, could adjust freely to the opportunities of American life; affiliation, largely voluntary, lacked the compulsive elements based on color. White Americans moved into a large number of separate organizations because they sensed, as individuals, needs best satisfied in terms of their differences.

The most significant differences had originated in the migrations that marked the history of the United States. In this society, the recollection of some displacement, from inside the country or from outside it, shaped the nature of men's cultures and indirectly of all their social activities.

It was very true, as Americans often remembered it, that they or their ancestors had all come, by land or by sea, from across some border. In a country that was always relatively new and in which social forms were very fluid, antecedents had considerable influence. Men of similar origins naturally clung together whether in the wilderness or among the strangenesses of the metropolitan centers.

The lines of ethnic descent therefore had a continuing impact upon the development of American society. There was an inclination toward occupational stratification as people with similar trainings from the old homes moved into the same pursuits, because they had brought across similar skills, or had access to common information, or enjoyed connections that made opportunities, or simply because they could trust each other. In a place where no religion was established, worshippers perpetuated inherited forms and those with identical heritages drew together. Specific memories of home could unite still others, as could old customs or the recollection of the pleasures of associational life. The expectation that, in a democracy, politics might serve the governed held others together. In a free society, people alike in their backgrounds moved together as a matter of course.

The influence of ethnic origin was clearest in the case of recent immigrants; but the same recollection of common antecedents extended also deep into the lives of folk for whom the decisive migration had been made by ancestors many generations back.

At the opening of the new century, of the sixty-five million Americans whom the census classified as white, only forty million were the children of native-born parents. The remainder, a substantial part of the whole, were either immigrants or the offspring of immigrants. And even among the forty million natives, a sizable percentage were the grandchildren of the newcomers of the 1840's and 1850's, grandchildren who had by no means lost consciousness of the nature of their ancestry. Yet this was not the full measure of the links of Americans with cultural sources outside their borders. The influence of such antecedents, among some individuals, within some groups, persisted in inherited patterns of thought and action for generation after generation, evidence of lines that stretched far beyond the immediate confines of the United States.

For two groups — the French-Canadians and Mexicans — in 1900 those lines were not figurative only. They were also geographical, reinforced by proximity to sources that permitted the free flow of individuals back and forth from the United States. For these immigrants, settlement in this country was simply an extension of life in their old homes and was substantially conditioned by that fact.

Shortly after the Civil War, large numbers of French-Canadians began to drift south across the border into New England to join the little colonies of refugees already there. The newcomers were mostly peasants or the sons of peasants, landless or without a place on the tiny farms of their parents. These immigrants increased rapidly in number with the peak of the movement in the decade after 1890. By 1900 there were almost 400,000 in the country as a whole, some three-fourths of them in New England, with smaller settlements in New York State, Michigan, Minnesota, and Montana. About 134,-000 lived in Massachusetts and 31,000 in Rhode Island. In New Hampshire (44,000) and Maine (31,000) the immigrants made up between 30 and 40 per cent of the population; and cities like Manchester, Lewiston, Biddeford, and Waterville had become almost solidly French-Canadian.

In New England, these people settled in towns where industry was expanding. The place they could not find on the land they discovered in the factories. Entering the mills first as unskilled laborers, sometimes as strikebreakers, they made themselves essential in manufacturing by virtue of the cheapness with which they sold their labor. But the price they paid was high. Their family incomes, of necessity, were made up of the wages of women and children as well as of those of the head of the household. Normally the large families lived meagerly in their cramped and dilapidated quarters. In good times, when all the earners worked, there might be money enough for spending beyond the bare necessities; but those periods were unhappily rare and did not long relieve the monotony and hardship of everyday existence.

These immigrants had left their close-knit little villages to

settle under altogether unfamiliar conditions. The earliest
comers back at the middle of the nineteenth century had
drifted, isolated, to places like Southbridge, Massachusetts,
where, dying alone, they were buried beside their Protestant
neighbors. But in time, in making such moves, they no longer
found it necessary to cut themselves off completely from the
ancient sources of their culture. Some were able to move
back and forth across the frontier, seasonally, in *l'émigration
vagabonde*. Visits became more common to the friends and
relatives who remained behind. On particular occasions it was
possible for whole groups to return for a festival at reduced
railroad fares. Others kept informed of occurrences in the
Quebec villages through new-coming acquaintances. The un-
interrupted flow of news and communications kept the old
homes constantly in contact with the new so that the French-
Canadians hardly felt conscious that the break in coming to
the United States was decisive or irrevocable. The mere
movement across the line of some map had not any cataclysmic cultural significance for them. As a result, they rarely
found it necessary to make their crossing permanent by
naturalization and found a thousand pretexts for not doing
so.

The influence of the link to Canada was pervasive. The
priests back home kept aware of the doings of their former
parishioners. In the 1880's, the French-Canadian clergy were
already concerned over the lack of the old family life in the
United States; and the migrants themselves sadly missed the
familiar institutions. They contrasted New England unfavor-
ably with Canada where every parish was "a circular horizon
with the church as a pivot." [1]

As soon as the growth of numbers supplied the means, the
French-Canadians attempted to reconstruct the traditional
environment. Catholics, they wished the precise forms of
their Catholicism to extend to their new homes. An excess of
zeal in that direction entangled them in difficulties with their

bishops who did not always understand the new leaven which had been added to American Catholicism, and with their Irish coreligionists in Portland, Maine, in North Brookfield, Massachusetts, or in Woonsocket, Rhode Island. Under such circumstances, the French-Canadians were sometimes inclined to heed the appeals of French-speaking missionaries or to send young people to the Franco-American College in Springfield, or to read the *Citoyen Franco-Américaine*, all Protestant efforts to make converts within the group. The only adequate safeguard against conversion was the rapid spread of Catholic churches with French-speaking priests.

But that action was not enough. It was necessary as well to transplant the round of holidays and festivals, to set aside a cemetery, and to organize religious fraternities. Indeed, the pattern of this life became more rigid in migration; what could be taken for granted at home had zealously to be fought for here. In Canada, widespread illiteracy had not seriously troubled anyone. In the United States educational requirements presented the newcomers with a double threat. In the existing parochial schools, their children would forget the ancestral language; in the public schools they would have training in neither language nor religion. The only solution was the creation of a new pattern of education to which instruction in French was central. By 1890 in Massachusetts, twenty-one thousand children were enrolled in such parochial schools; and determined efforts were thereafter made to assure the inclusion of the "maternal language" in the public school curriculum throughout New England.

In the last decades of the nineteenth century a group of leaders among these immigrants sought to give the community a more formal organization. In little *cercles canadiens*, the shopkeeper, the foreman, the lawyer, and the pharmacist considered the situation of their compatriots. These people strove to devise the means of preserving their French identity and of asserting themselves in the larger American society in which they lived. They faced the fact that they were in the United States to stay; and they busied themselves with a variety of institutions to assist the adjustment. Their efforts might take the form of a banking coöperative as in Manchester, New Hampshire, in 1905, or of a literary and dramatic society, or of a musical group, or of associations to promote contacts with the homeland, to relieve the poor, to encourage temperance, and to teach English to candidates for naturalization.

The activity which evoked most support however was that of the mutual aid societies which touched closely the intimate needs of the immigrants. Such societies, fraternal and benevolent in their functions, had developed autonomously in almost every town; by 1891, there were more than three hundred and fifty with a combined membership of almost fifty thousand. Efforts to give a central organization to the group led to the formation of a number of loose national federations with which the local bodies affiliated. The first (1896), L'Association Canada-Américaine had its headquarters in Manchester, New Hampshire. Its rival, L'Union Saint-Jean-Baptiste d'Amérique (1900), operated out of Woonsocket, Rhode Island. And a number of French "courts" of the Ancient Order of Foresters seceded in 1905 to form L'Ordre des Forestiers franco-américaine when the parent body insisted upon the use of English as the official language.

The attempts to establish a French-Canadian press were less immediately successful. These papers depended for support upon people who had not earlier been accustomed to reading newspapers, who were often illiterate, who lived in small towns where local news passed quickly by word of mouth, and who had easy access, if they wished it, to journals published in Quebec. Nevertheless there were frequent efforts to established local newspapers. By 1900, among the more prominent were *Le Messager* in Lewiston, Maine, *L'Opinion Publique* in Worcester, and *L'Étoile* in Lowell, Massachusetts.

By this time too, the leaders of the community had perceived the importance of advancing themselves politically. There were repeated exhortations concerning the importance of naturalization and of the exercise of the ballot. A few individuals, with the aid of the new voters, rose to the dignity of local officeholders, and Aram J. Pothier in 1908 attained the gubernatorial chair of Rhode Island.

The French-Canadian communities in the United States drew strength from two closely related sources. The proximity to the old homeland, the fact that the new settlements were under the constant oversight of the villages in Quebec, supplied moral sanctions that held the group together. And precisely because the group held together, its settlement was concentrated in the compact mill towns of New England, where a tight communal life developed. There were scattered outposts in Detroit, Buffalo, and Chicago; but the overwhelming majority of the French-Canadians insisted on staying in the region closest to their native land. Indeed, that insistence by 1910 was limiting the capacity of the group to grow. As the great areas of industrial expansion shifted to cities in the western and middle states, the French-Canadian, tied to New England, found his opportunities contracting. The strength of his ties across the border kept him where he was. Furthermore, the conscious opposition of the hierarchy in Quebec reduced the volume of Canadian emigration. There was therefore no substantial overflow beyond the boundaries of the Northeastern states.

When the new century opened, a similar migration from across the southern border was about to alter the life of another section of the country. As the railroad penetrated through western Texas, Colorado, Arizona, and California, and as seasonal commercial agriculture took hold through the 1890's, the cultivators of cotton, citrus fruits, and vegetables looked with eagerness for new recruits for their potential labor force. Some hoped that the Negroes would take a place in these fields too, others saw the solution to their problems in Oriental pickers, and still others in European immigrants. But Negroes and Europeans regarded the industrial North as their promised land; and social complications and ultimate exclusion stood in the way of more extensive employment of Orientals.

It was therefore the immigrants from Mexico who entered ever more prominently upon these tasks. Attracted from their villages, they moved north across the Rio Grande, migrating with the alternation of crops through field after field of the West, and seasonally returning to their old homes. In time considerable numbers were permanently fixed as residents of the United States, perhaps one hundred thousand in 1900, perhaps as many as 220,000 in 1910. In time, too, the circle of their migrations reached as far north as the beet fields of Michigan, and some entered the more settled employment of the railroads and mines.

The Mexicans, like the French-Canadians, did not readily shed the influence of their antecedents. Coming into areas already acutely sensitive to race differences from experience with Negroes and Orientals, they were often accorded inferior treatment. Although not clearly identified with the blacks, they were barred from many public facilities, in some places refused burial in "white" cemeteries or admission to "white" schools. Nor could the newcomers establish an advantageous relationship with the Hispanos, the descendants of those settled on the land before the war of 1846. The old inhabitants, often themselves marginal peasants, nevertheless rejected the poorer migrants, who lowered all Spanish-speaking peoples in the eyes of the Anglos.

The continued vitality of ties across the border constantly reminded the Mexicans who they were. They had brought with them language and peculiarities of diet, festivals and a persistent longing for *mi tierra*, that were signs of their continued affiliation with the homeland. On the other hand they were not by 1914 able to create the stable communal life that the French-Canadians had. They were fewer in numbers, perhaps poorer, and had not been as long in the country. Furthermore, the migratory nature of their labor kept them from the attachment to fixed places that might have supplied the context for communal life in America. Nor, shifting about as they did, could they educate a second generation from which leadership might come. More decisively even than the French-Canadians, these people were held together only by the connections they still felt with the source of their culture across the border.

All immigrants longed for home. But some had not the easy access to it of those whose migration consisted only of a short trip by land. The intervening ocean that cut the Europeans off from their familiar villages was a more imposing divide. Some such newcomers would ultimately go back to the place of their birth for temporary visits or in a permanent return. But the vast majority of those who came by sea could not afford the expense, or the time, could not easily undertake the hardships of more than one crossing. For these people migration was a decisive step that rarely involved a series of departures and arrivals.

Europeans in the New World were, therefore, thrown more upon their own resources. For some time, as long as the flow continued, new immigrants would still bring with them the elements of the familiar culture, and would thereby renew the connections between their countrymen in America and the homeland. But those newcomers themselves would be entering groups that were adjusting gradually to the terms of the American environment. And eventually, for all, an end would come to the arrivals. Then adjustment would be entirely on the basis of American conditions.

That point was still remote for some Europeans. In the two

decades before 1917, the third great wave of American immigration had brought to the United States millions of new
residents who sought the means of being at home in a strange
society. Along the shores of the Mediterranean and in the
eastern reaches of the continent, the effects of industrial and
agricultural change, only just being felt as the nineteenth
century ended, were unloosing a mass of displaced peasants
between 1890 and 1914. The host of migrants from these
areas would find few predecessors of their own kind to meet
them here, and they would create afresh the cultural and
social institutions that gave meaning to their lives. To outsiders all these people seemed to duplicate each other's
efforts; but the multiplicity and confusion of organizations
was only the product of each man's certainty that his own
transplanted situation was unique.

The tabulators of immigration and census statistics would
long have difficulty in classifying these foreigners, who often
themselves could not say to what country they belonged. In
Portugal, in Italy, in Turkey, in Austria, Russia, or Germany,
these men had been the subjects of monarchs. But that subjection had by no means endowed them with any sense of
participation in the state or given them a feeling of national
identity. Fixed for centuries, they thought of themselves
mostly in the simple terms of their own village circle, within
which they were at home and outside of which were only
strangers. Yet they could not transplant the village to the
New World; in vain the migrants attempted to cling to the
institutions they had known. Invariably they discovered that
life in the United States made demands of its own to which
the old forms were inadequate. The urge to worship God in
their own fashion, to guard against the contingencies of death
or illness, to exchange the confidences of friendship, drew
them together in groups far larger than any they had participated in at home. In the formation of those groups a variety
of elements were influential — common language, common

religion, and the recollection of old grievances. But mostly the nature of their affiliations was shaped by the nature of their settlement in the United States. For it was only the experience of living in a strange society that taught them how to unite in the achievement of their common objectives.

The movement out of Italy had not really begun until after 1880. Before that date a handful of priests, of intellectuals, and of merchants had made their appearance in the United States. But as the century drew to a close a mass of displaced peasants, uprooted by changes in the agricultural economy of the peninsula, sought new lives in America. By 1900, some 484,000 were already here.

In the next decade, almost two million more Italians debarked in the receiving stations of New York, Boston, and New Orleans. Not all stayed: some, after an unfortunate trial of fortune, gave up to return to their disappointed families; others quickly found the means of accumulating by their labor the funds to take them back to their villages. But by 1910 enough had remained so that the census counted 1,343,-000 Italians in the United States. With their native-born children they formed a community of well over two million eager to reconstruct a way of life in America.

Although almost all these newcomers had lived on the soil in Italy, relatively few found places in American agriculture. Some labored on the great fruit farms of the Pacific coast, others made an adjustment in tiny rural settlements in Illinois, Louisiana, California, Georgia, New York, and New England. But for most the capital necessary to start an American farm was large, out of reach.

A handful found places that involved some independent skill — as bootblacks and barbers and in the other service occupations — but most Italians drifted into the ranks of industry. In the big cities contractors mobilized them in the back-breaking jobs of the building trades; elsewhere the foremen in mines and mills assigned them the harshest labor.

At their arrival, the peasants thought of themselves, as they had at home, in terms of village *campanilismo*. Always their interests had been local, limited to the little area within the shadow of their own church tower, so that even a man from only a few miles away was distinguishable in dialect and costume. In the United States those who had known each other in the Old Country were likely to take up the same occupation — the New York icemen were all Apulians, the knife grinders natives of Campobasso — and were also likely to cluster together in residence. In shaping their institutions, they gave first attention to what had been most local and most familiar.

The *festa*, the annual commemoration of the patron saint of a particular place, was, therefore, as important in the New World as it had been in the Old. Back in 1881 in New York, a group of emigrants from Polla near Salerno had determined that distant as they were Our Lady of Mount Carmel should have her due. So, in time, the Catanians would remember Sant-Agata; Sicilians would express their gratitude to Santa Rosalia who once had saved Palermo from destruction; and Neapolitans would discover the climax of their year in the day of San Gennaro. Even those who, by the choice prosperity gave them or by the necessities of the job, moved away from their fellows eagerly came back to the neighborhood for these celebrations.

Here it was true the day was not whole; making a living left not that much time for leisure. Nor was there an equivalent in America for the familiar setting, the trim and ordered landscape, clear in the light of the long Italian sun. Still, along the lit-up block where the cries of the hawkers and the irrepressible noise of youngsters up beyond all bedtime mingled in melody with mandolin and accordion, sound and color shut out the ugly lineaments of the everyday houses. The community could draw away from the outsiders in the silent, somber darkness of the street beyond, and find an equivalent that gave value to their being together.

It was quite different in the churches. There the evidences of foreignness crowded in upon them. Catholics mostly, the Italians found the Church already in existence in the cities to which they came. But the church was not theirs. Built by other worshippers, the priests, the saints, the names, the very language was unfamiliar. Like the French-Canadians, the immigrants from Italy struggled long to attain some elements of control that would enable them to rebuild the church in the image of what they had known in the Old Country.

The bishops often resisted, strengthened now by the earlier failure of the Cahenslyite agitation to secure a reorganization of the Church in the United States along national lines. Sometimes long, acrimonious controversies ensued, or outright secession as in the case of the San Marco Society in Boston. But ultimately the new immigrants gained the ascendancy in parishes in which their numbers grew to a preponderance.

The hierarchy could not help but accommodate itself to the presence of this group, for allegiance could only be held voluntarily. Antagonized, the Italians might be lost to the faith entirely. Certainly in the first decades of the twentieth century the Protestant denominations were alive to the possibility of proselytizing among the disaffected. Episcopalians, Methodists, and Presbyterians set up missions in the Italian quarters of the cities and sponsored itinerant evangelists to work among the newcomers in the small towns. Such ministers as Antonio Arrighi, Michele Nardi, and Giuseppe A. Villelli, who spoke the old tongue and knew the Old Country, were less strange often than the pastors of the Catholic church. And the Protestants might attract the immigrants, or their children, by their greater social prestige and by the hope that conversion would raise the level of the whole group in American society.

Still a greater danger to the traditional ways sprang from within. Intellectuals and professionals, few in number, were a stronger influence. Literate, more prosperous than the bulk of their fellows, and more capable of dealing with the American environment, they were in a position to assume the leadership of their countrymen. From the generation of Mazzini they had inherited both a strong national consciousness and an ideology of anti-clericalism through which they expressed the current grievances of the Italians.

A smaller nucleus of radicals attempted to draw the Italian-Americans into the extreme wing of the labor movement. Neglected by the craft unions and made desperate by miserable conditions, the Italian workers in times of crisis often found no one willing to speak their case but the ultra-radicals. Thus a handful of men like Giovannitti and Ettor in the I.W.W. were able to assume the direction of strikes in Paterson and Lawrence and to act for a time as spokesmen for the entire group.

The various anarchists and socialists joined to their schemes of social reconstruction a thoroughgoing atheism. They would continue to have a voice in Italian-American affairs for several decades. But they were incapable of sustaining their own influence. Fundamentally, there was a marked antipathy between their radicalism or liberalism and the conservative peasant ideas of the mass of Italian immigrants, who only listened to anti-clerical accusations while they had their own grievances against the Church. Yet the peasants wished, not to destroy the Church, but to reconstruct it. While they were often discontented, they gradually accepted in practice compromises that promised to bring the Church back to them.

The restoration never was complete. The new life was too fluid to permit the indefinite perpetuation of the old village attachments. Instead immigrants found themselves drawn together by a larger affiliation the basis of which was the language that permitted them to communicate with each other.

The churches became not Palermian or Apulian, but Italian. The *festa* widened until there was room in it for Italians from a whole province, and ultimately the basis for participation shifted from the village in the Old Country to the neighborhood in the New. In the little eating places and the cafes where the men stopped by, the styles of food came to mingle incongruously every regional specialty; dishes from Sicily and Bologna met in America in a gastronomic rapport unknown back home.

In other social activities also, American experience taught these people to disregard the differences in dialect and custom among the various *paesani*. In meeting the problems of insecurity and loneliness of life in the United States, these immigrants had turned first to thousands of local spontaneous societies, within which they could offer each other mutual aid and comradeship. By the opening of the new century a growing number of middle-class and professional folk, themselves once peasants or the children of peasants, had become familiar with American ideas and were anxious to weld the group into a more effective unit. After much consideration, a clique of such doctors, pharmacists, teachers, and lawyers, not unlike the type of clique that had begun to lead the French-Canadians, in 1905 founded the Order of the Sons of Italy in America. Within six years the Order had spread until it had sixty-seven lodges and it continued to expand despite secessions and occasional internal conflicts. By this time also the Italian language press had produced a number of dailies with large circulations, further evidence of the self-consciousness and developing organization of the Italians as a group.

Often in the American mills and mines or in the quarters of the cities they had made their own, the Italians encountered a mass of other immigrants from southern and eastern Europe whom outsiders considered all of a kind. They were not; divided among themselves by languages and religion, they were beginning to draw together into tentative groups of their own.

The process of adjustment through which these people passed was essentially the same as that of the Italians. Generally, whether they came from Epirus or the Azores, from Galicia or Smyrna, they were peasants; and most often in the United States they became industrial workers. Invariably, they attempted to live their own lives through their familiar church and within traditional communities and invariably in America they found themselves drawn into larger spheres of action.

At first, these people, being strangers, could exercise little choice as to what church or lodge they could join; they fell in with the closest available approximation. But as they grew in numbers, they acquired the capacity to suit their local peculiarities more accurately. Secessions and schisms then marked the elaboration of their associational life. The intellectuals and professional people among them, influenced by the desire to make a mark in the United States and by the nationalist ideas they encountered on both sides of the Atlantic, attempted to give these divisions a national form and to tie into large units the myriad local societies that were constantly springing up everywhere. To hold the loyalty of their communicants, the churches fell in with the same tendency. Invariably, therefore, the immigrants fell into groups, each served by Sokols and benevolent societies, secular and clerical, and by its own churches. Sometimes a common language united the newcomers from the start. At other times, as the press and schools developed, the numerous dialects that shaded off into each other in their spoken forms, were formalized for the mass of immigrants into separate languages. And ultimately all would establish connections with movements back in Europe which would seem to root them in the Old World.

Utimately, the immigrants would describe themselves as

Portuguese, Greeks, Albanians, Syrians, Armenians, Poles, and Lithuanians. But these were not clear-cut designations in existence from the start. Rather they described affiliations worked out in the course of settlement.

From the Atlantic Islands and from Portugal, there had long been a substantial movement in whaling ships and in small packets of laborers, drawn mostly to New England where they worked in the textile mills, the fisheries, and the cranberry bogs. Coming from places with a long history of intermarriage among Negroes, Moors, and Iberians, these newcomers were distinguished by marked differences of color and by strong local sentiments. The Bravas, former residents of the Cape Verde Islands, were almost black, while the emigrants from the Azores, Madeiras, and from the Portuguese mainland were lighter in pigmentation. Immigration statistics ultimately recognized that distinction by classing the first-named as Africans, the rest as Europeans.

In the early stages of their life in America these people were chaotically disorganized. In Boston they were long compelled to share a Roman Catholic church with the Italians. Not a few were undoubtedly absorbed within the growing Italian community. Some others, darker in color, threw in their lot with the Negroes. But in places like New Bedford, Fall River, Gloucester, and on Cape Cod, where they formed concentrated settlements, a common economic and social situation and similarity of customs permitted them to build up associations that centered in the language they all spoke. By 1910, the census revealed that some 140,000 — foreign-born or the children of foreign-born — thus identified themselves as Portuguese.

A simultaneous process of immigration originated at the other end of the Mediterranean. In the 1890's, peasants were on their way from Macedonia, the Ionian Islands, Crete, Epirus, Thrace, and Turkey. Set in motion by a blight of the currant crop, this movement was the product of the same

economic displacements that were also transforming other
parts of Europe, although discrimination by the Turkish
Government after 1908 added political and religious incentives. The mass of these newcomers fell into unskilled occupations, labored in the textile mills and fisheries of New England, in the railroads and lumber mills of the West, in the
mines of Colorado, in the slaughterhouses of Chicago, in the
steel mills of Akron and Youngstown, Ohio, in the hotels,
shoeshine parlors, and amusement places of New York, in
the vineyards of California, and in the sponge fisheries of
Florida. With these peasants came a handful of intellectuals
and businessmen engaged in shipping and in the tobacco
industries.

As with other newcomers, the first associations were local,
and ties to the native village long remained strong. As with
the others again, however, American life imposed the necessity of some larger affiliation. These people found in the
United States no churches in which they could worship. That
posed at once the problem of making some religious provision for themselves. Under the influence of the Turkish
practice, they thought of themselves as Greeks, a term that
described not their language but their status as Orthodox
Christians, which they shared with folk in many other parts
of eastern Europe and Asia Minor. To bring to America the
priests who could minister to them the immigrants had, back
in the 1880's, begun to form "Slavo-Hellenic" unions that
took in all those in the Orthodox communion, whether they
spoke Greek, Russian, or Bulgarian.

The experience of strangers in the new society however
kept raising the question of what was their identity. Expansion in numbers encouraged a clearer answer, for it made
possible institutions to which the Greek language was central.
Shaking off Russian connections, Orthodox churches could
use Greek, could preserve traditional customs, and could
maintain a spiritual relationship to the Metropolitan Arch-

bishop of Athens. Afternoon schools encouraged young people to acquire the language and the culture of their parents and developed familiarity with the civilization and problems of the old land.

The influence of the intellectuals and business people helped transform the old local loyalties into an awareness of a more general Greek identity. These people had been conscious of their nationality before they emigrated; they sprang from social groups which in the Old World had been most involved in nationalist movements. In America their situation as leaders gave them an interest in encouraging the sense of cohesiveness of those who might be their followers: and they desired to do so in a form comprehensible to Americans, attachment not to the local village, not even to Trace or Epirus, but to a national state — Greece.

The mass of immigrants were consequently urged to unite, both to better their conditions in the United States and to support the homeland — although many of them never had been citizens of Greece. On the first score they were urged to become naturalized Americans and to take part in politics. On the second they were encouraged to develop Hellenic societies in accord with the injunction of Prince George who had passed through the United States in 1891. The newspapers were particularly active in this respect, the dailies *Atlantis* and *Pan Hellenic* (started 1894 and 1904), as well as weeklies published in Boston, Lowell, Lynn, Manchester, Pittsburgh, Chicago, Salt Lake City, and San Francisco.

The mutual aid societies therefore quickly fell into a nationalistic form. The Pan Hellenic Union, established in 1907, within five years had twenty thousand members in one hundred and fifty branches. The Union heatedly took sides as the bitter conflict over Macedonia developed into war against Turkey and Bulgaria. In 1912, it encouraged immigrants to return to fight for Greece, and supplied funds for those who did so. By that time the 130,000 American Greeks of the first and second generations had no doubts as to what their affiliations were.

Other immigrants from the eastern Mediterranean, mostly subjects of the Sultan, passed through a similar process of definition. Some no doubt never managed to find a satisfactory affiliation, or shifted from one to another, or like the Macedonians, Turks, and Assyrians, formed lonely little cliques wherever a few gathered. But by 1914 three substantial nationalities — Armenian, Syrian, Albanian — had been delineated, each embracing some fifty to one hundred thousand Americans.

Among the Armenians were a rather unusual number of business people with capital, induced to leave by the massacres of 1894. With the humbler laborers who went to the mills and vineyards, they settled in the Eastern cities and in a Western outpost in Fresno, California. The high literacy rate and the large percentage of men with commercial skills enabled many to prosper quickly without the difficulties of economic adjustment other immigrants encountered.

These people had come mostly from Turkish and Russian Armenia, although there were sprinklings from Egypt, Romania, and elsewhere. Almost all were united by a distinctive language; and those who were not, the Turkish-speaking natives of Adana and Caesarea, were communicants of the Church of Armenia, acknowledging the authority of its Catholicos. As a minority even at home, they were, to begin with, conscious of their separate identity and in America drew together as a matter of course. Significantly, they frequently joined branches of the Armenian Benevolent Union founded in 1906 in Cairo.

Distinctiveness of language in the case of the Syrians proved more important than sharp religious differences. The immigrants in the 1890's from the Turkish province of Syria included a great variety of men — peasants, laborers, and traders — who went to work in American mills or earned a competence as peddlers. They brought with them faiths strange to America; they were Melkite or Maronite Catholics, Moslems, Druzes, Protestants, or communicants of the Orthodox churches. The link that bound these people together was a language, Arabic, remote from every other American tongue. A common medium of communication made them readers of the same newspapers and brought them together first in local societies named after the town of origin and then in a United Syrian Organization. It was thus they learned to identify themselves.

The immigrants from the southern shores of the Adriatic, who at home called themselves Shqipetare, in the United States might, if they were Orthodox, have fallen in with the Greeks, or, if they were Mohammedans, with the Bosnians or Serbs. No doubt some of them did. But through the influence of two forceful personalities, a substantial number in eastern and central Massachusetts learned to consider themselves Albanians.

Into the crowded *konak*, the communal tenement in which these humble mill workers lived, or into the halls where their local fraternal societies met, there may have penetrated some word that intellectuals in Bucharest or Cairo were spinning theories of an Albanian nation and language. But such notions could not have had much meaning for these subjects of the Sultan until 1908 and 1909. Those were the years in which Fan Sylian Noli and Faik Bey Konitza reached Boston. Both were well-to-do; Konitza, having studied at Paris, had come to work in Harvard. They were seized with a missionary zeal, to teach the people who did not yet know it that they were Albanian, and to make them familiar with an ancient language they hardly understood.

Four measures furthered that end. Noli created the Autocephalous Albanian Orthodox Church, with himself its first bishop. Konitza established *Dielli*, an Albanian newspaper. Together they drew the fraternal societies into *Vatra*, a fed-

eration that would prove a useful tool in their hands. And,
as if to reward their efforts, the Great Powers, intervening
after the first Balkan War in 1912, prevented Serbia from
taking their mountainous homeland away from Turkey, and
instead made Albania an independent state, a nation to which
they could thereafter attach their loyalty.

The millions who left for America from central and eastern
Europe passed through an analogous process of self-discovery.
They too had been villagers, had been displaced by the same
forces that had operated along the Mediterranean, and in the
United States they encountered the same problems of economic and social adjustment. If anything, their problems
were more complicated because the regions they left had for
centuries been conquered and reconquered, passed from beneath the suzerainty of one empire to another. History had
left few places in this area homogeneous; everywhere variations in language and religion and custom marked off district
from district. Like the Italians and the Greeks, the people
who would come to know themselves as Poles and Slovenes
would arrive at that knowledge mainly through their experience in the New World.

In the middle of the nineteenth century a scattering of intellectuals had come to the United States from Posen, Silesia,
and Galicia, the vanguard of the mass migration out of the
same regions that would follow three decades later. At first,
these intellectuals had found a place for themselves in the life
of the German-Americans. After the revolution of 1863,
however, a substantial number became more conscious of the
particular Polish national aims. The consciousness was expressed in 1880 when a group of political refugees founded
the Polish National Alliance of North America.

The peasants who came to the United States between 1890
and 1914 from the sections of Austria, Germany, and Russia
that had more than a century earlier formed the kingdom of
Poland had migrated because there was no place for them on

the old land. They had had little concern with the nationalistic furor that moved some intellectuals and noblemen to labor for the restoration of the ancient state. The preoccupations of the immigrants were with economic problems, with the transition from labor on the soil to unskilled toil in the mills and mines. Beyond that, their thoughts went, as had those of the Italians, to restoration of their churches, to mutual assistance, and to the preservation of village custom.

To attempt to preserve inevitably meant to change, however. The early comers often found it necessary to worship in German Catholic churches or, when they formed their own, to be served by priests who did not speak the old language. The immigrants therefore put much energy into the drive to create a more familiar church, among the extremists in the form of the schismatic Polish National Church, among the majority in separate Catholic parishes. In both cases, the emphasis on language gradually outlined the Polish character of those who affiliated with the group.

Meanwhile, the Polish Alliance, already functioning when the great migration of the 1890's got under way, tended to absorb the local benevolent societies which the new immigrants themselves had set up. By 1909, the Alliance had more than a thousand branches and more than 60,000 members; and its newspaper *Zgoda* actively spread the gospel of a reborn Poland. To that end the association also sponsored supplementary language schools in many places and set up Alliance College in Pennsylvania in 1912.

The anti-clericalism of the Alliance and the nationalism of the schismatics compelled the Catholic Church to struggle for the loyalty of these immigrants. It had to acknowledge the national separateness of the group, indeed to emphasize the Catholic quality of Polonia. It organized benevolent associations parallel to the Alliance, and sponsored parochial schools, hospitals, orphanages, and homes for the aged which confirmed not only the religious, but even more, the national identity of the participants. New connections with its place of origin heightened the group's self-consciousness. The Order of the Falcons spread to the United States and absorbed many Americans in an organization whose headquarters were in Europe. Nationalistic leaders like Paderewski, lecturing here, worked to involve the immigrant in the struggle for an independent Poland.

While to the end of their days many still referred to themselves in village terms, or continued to call themselves Germans, Austrians, or Russians, nevertheless a cohesive Polish group steadily evolved which learned to think itself tied to a particular nation; one not yet in existence, it was true, but characterized by common language and culture. In 1900, perhaps four hundred thousand thus identified themselves. How many more immigrated in the next ten years cannot be known. But, in the census of 1910, a million foreign-born and seven hundred thousand native-born put themselves into the category of Poles.

In a similar development, the Bohemians in the United States had already broken away from their early German affiliations and established their own group life. Shortly after the middle of the nineteenth century, small coteries of romantic intellectuals, themselves schooled in the German tradition, had rediscovered the Slavonic sources of their culture and had begun to convert the growing number of immigrants to the use of the Czech language. Largely freethinkers, they centered their activities in St. Louis and Chicago and made their most substantial appeal to the more prosperous Western settlers.

In the East, where former peasants employed in mines and factories predominated, the influence of the Catholic Church was stronger. But the Church here too made concessions to separatist inclinations. The result was a twofold pull through benevolent societies, Sokols, and the press under both church and freethinking auspices that drew many Austrians, Bohe-

mians, and Moravians in a nationalistic direction to the consciousness that they were Czechs. By 1910 in this group, there
were some two hundred thousand foreign-born and three
hundred thousand natives.

In that year there were perhaps a million more Americans
who acknowledged ties of birth to other parts of eastern
Europe. After 1890 the process of Americanization had defined a succession of smaller groups among them. So the
Lithuanians began to count themselves apart from the Poles;
the Slovaks did the same. The Ruthenians moved out of an
affiliation with the Slovaks. The Ukrainians and Little Russians separated themselves from the Poles and Slovaks to form
organizations of their own. Croatians, Slovenians, Great Russians, Bulgarians, Serbians, Reinanians, and Magyars similarly
acquired a consciousness of national identity. Each group
had its quota of benevolent associations, newspapers, and
churches. Each was also divided by religious differences,
political dissension, and factionalism. Often the groups over-
lapped, and as often they left substantial numbers of immigrants without any affiliation; for both reasons, there was a
wide diversity to the guesses at their size. But whatever their
form or size, these were meaningful reactions to life in the
United States which called for a kind of community wider
than had been familiar in the old villages of home.

The departure of the peasants of central and eastern Europe
upset every other element of the population that lived with
them. Many people, dependent for their own livelihood on
services to the husbandmen, found themselves superfluous
and, in their turn, were compelled to emigrate.

The Jews in these regions had been middlemen, either intermediaries between the peasants and landlords or traders in a
society of agriculturists. Their role disappeared when large-
scale commercial farms displaced the old peasant holdings.
Since the Jewish population of Europe was in any case increasing rapidly, large numbers were left with nothing to do,

and had no recourse but to move. They joined a smaller flock
of migrants already in motion as a result of religious perse-
cutions in Russia after 1880. Coming directly to America or
after brief experiences as a proletariat in the factories of
England or of the Polish provinces, they took up a strange
new life. In the twenty years after 1890, there were about
a million such immigrants; with them by 1910 were some six
hundred thousand native-born children.

Largely unskilled in terms of the immediate needs of the
American economy, these people drifted as laborers into light
manufacturing, particularly into the expanding clothing industries. Because of that concentration they clustered in the
large cities where such work was available; about one-half
lived in New York and there were large nuclei also in Boston,
Philadelphia, and Chicago.

Like other immigrants, they created at once their own
institutional life. Small groups of neighbors from the old
home assembled in synagogues or in societies to visit the sick,
to bury the dead, and to aid the indigent. They too devised
fraternal and social orders often centering about the extended
family group or the *landsmannschaft*, an association based on
the region of emigration. Throughout this period, organizations retained that local character; as much as they were Jews,
these people were also Galicians or Lithuanians or Bessara-
bians, divided by differences in dialect, in the order of religious services, and in customs.

But it was difficult to act like a Galician or Lithuanian. As
the immigrant groupings took form, the Jews sometimes
participated in the associations of their Christian fellow-
countrymen. They took an active part in the Russian-Ameri-
can League, in the Hungarian and Romanian and Bohemian
societies, even in the publication of Polish newspapers. There
were subtle barriers in the way of full integration, however.
Jews and peasants both had brought with them from the Old
World a sense of their separateness; and since religion played

so dominant a part in the constitution of these societies, dissenting groups could never fully share their life.

As Jews moved away from the districts of first residence, or as they changed occupations, they found inadequate the early local societies; but they saw little to attract them in the developing Polish or Romanian or Russian national organizations. For a time, the Jews attempted to form similar associations on their own religious basis, a federation of Polish Jews, for instance, and a union of Romanian Jews. But the conditions of Jewish life in the United States gave their community another form.

Common language and common economic situation were the cohesive influences. The immigrants all spoke Yiddish, but they had brought with them variations of dialect that clearly marked off the tongue of one region from that of another. In the New World these Jews developed an American Yiddish. The urge to appeal to as wide an audience as possible moved the newspapers to impose a uniformity upon the written language, and the theater upon the spoken. The steady intrusion of English words and forms tended to minimize peculiarities inherited from Europe and served to draw all Yiddish-speaking Jews together.

The high concentration of employment in a few industries and of residence in a few cities had a similar effect. In the early days, the homeworkers or those who came to the shop of the small contractor might all be neighbors from the same town back home. But as the units of production grew larger and as individuals changed their trades, these distinctions were wiped out. The labor movement developed within the lines of the Yiddish-speaking Jewish group. The emerging unions themselves and, more important, the ancillary benevolent and educational organizations such as the United Hebrew Trades and the Workingmen's Circle emphasized the identity and the unity of these eastern European Jews.

Other Jews, whether long settled in the country or newcomers from other parts of the world, did not then enter the east European community. The handful who were migrating in these years from Morocco, Greece, and Asia Minor remained a group apart; differences of language, ritual, and economic adjustment gave them identities of their own.

The eastern Europeans also maintained their distance from the Jews already established in the United States, who, whatever their actual antecedents, were by contrast known as Germans. Some 300,000 strong when the great influx of the 1880's began, the German Jews had adjusted on relatively favorable terms to the life of the New World. They had risen to positions in trade that put them economically well above the newcomers. They had developed charitable and social institutions adequate to their own needs. Their religion had come to terms with the American environment; by 1900, reform had surrendered the Sabbath, adopted English as the language of worship, and discarded the conception of exile. Approaching the forms of Protestantism, some among them even anticipated a period when Judaism would develop into a kind of Unitarianism. Under these circumstances there was little common ground with the Jews of eastern Europe.

That there was any common ground at all was due to three factors. Concern with the fate of their unfortunate coreligionists elsewhere was a tie that drew all American Jews together. Persecution and discrimination under the Czar and Sultan led to protests and active organization for defense, not only among the recent comers with kin overseas, but also among the German Jews who in 1906 formed the American Jewish Committee for that purpose.

In addition, Jews like other Americans were heirs to the old tradition of the oneness of the children of Jacob and of a purpose in their long mysterious survival. For Christians that purpose was providential — evidence of the truth of the Scriptures until the Second Coming which their conversion would behold. For Orthodox Jews the purpose of survival was a messianic return to the Holy Land; while the reformed viewed it as the means for the diffusion of the ethical ideals of monotheism.

Finally, the continuing flow of new immigrants tempted the already-settled with the prospect of recruits. The minority of German Jews still Orthodox and organized through the Jewish Theological Seminary and the developing Conservative movement hoped that the newcomers, properly Americanized, would help stem the tide of reform. The Reform leaders, finding difficulty in training up ministers from the children of their own communicants, thought they might do so from among children of east Europeans. And the remaining descendants of the old Sephardic Jews, long outnumbered by the Germans, saw in the oriental Jews the means of reviving their distinctive religious forms. Thus there was a basis for the approaching *rapprochement* between old German and new east European Jews. But 1914 still found a distinct line between the two groups.

Other immigrants in the same years were spared the difficulties of creating a fresh institutional life because they could move into communities they found already functioning when they arrived. The decade after 1900 thus saw well over three hundred thousand newcomers from Germany join the three million here at the opening of the century. But the process of self-discovery had been long completed for them; their adjustment would be in terms of forms by then well established.

Displaced peasants and artisans from the German parts of central Europe, who had been coming to the United States since early in the nineteenth century, swept *en masse* across the Atlantic in two great waves in the 1850's and 1880's. By 1900 these people and their descendants had made their adjustments, found their means of livelihood, settled in cities, towns, and on farms, and built the kinds of Catholic and

Lutheran churches they desired. By then too, they had lived through the internal dissensions that had once divided province against province, grays against greens, and *hochdeutsch* against *plattdeutsch*. Social institutions, a common language evolving through the press and the theater, and the influence of the nationalist exiles of mid-century had drawn them all together as Germans. The high esteem in which Americans held German culture and the emergence of the Empire as a great power increased the sense of cohesion. By the end of the century that feeling had shaken the Catholic Church with the demand for dioceses organized according to nationalities and had also created separate branches and locals within the anarchist, socialist, and labor movements.

The immigrants who came across after 1900 had grown up since the establishment of the Empire and had been subjected to the universal education and the nationalizing influences that imparted to them acute awareness of their German identity. They fell without difficulty into the pattern of life set by their predecessors. By 1910 the German-Americans formed a community of well over six million.

More than 300,000 immigrants from Ireland, like those from Germany, moved between 1900 and 1910 into a community already well-organized. There was hardly a distinction between late and early comers. For more than sixty years the movement out of the Emerald Isle had had a single character, the product of the elimination of a numerous displaced peasantry. Continuity of adjustment also held Irishmen together; they made a start in the same unskilled occupations, and worshipped in the same church since American Catholicism had long since acquired an Irish cast. The last to arrive moved into well-established societies and shared places with their predecessors or their children. Some stratification along economic lines reflected the ability of members of the second and third generations to earn the incomes and move to the districts where they might live their lace-curtain lives. But even that mobility did not altogether destroy the sense of identity that reached back to take in alike the newest arrivals and the descendants of immigrants who had come to America almost a century back.*

Something over 400,000 immigrants arrived from the Scandinavian countries in the fifteen years after 1900. They joined in the United States two and a half million earlier comers and their descendants. Those who settled with people from their own districts on the farms of Wisconsin or Minnesota or North Dakota had no difficulty fitting themselves into communities already in existence, communities which centered in old village ties but which by now had become identified as Norwegian, Danish, and Swedish through the development of associations and newspapers oriented around distinctions of language or religion. Others who settled in such places as Chicago, or Minneapolis, or Brooklyn, or Worcester, where substantial numbers of their fellows clustered, could exercise almost as wide a choice. And even where there were no marked concentrations, there was almost everywhere an available approximation: Lutheranism here and there drew some into German communities; and elsewhere the needs of association blurred the peculiarities among Dane and Swede and Norwegian. It was in recognition of these common elements that Nils Poulsen organized the American Scandinavian Foundation in 1911.

Smaller groups of Swiss, Finns, and Hollanders made the same adjustment. Scattered individuals found enough points of religious, linguistic, and cultural similarity to fit themselves into Italian, French, Swedish, Russian, or German

---

* In the case of the Irish-Americans it is impossible to make even an approximately accurate guess of numbers. There were 1,300,000 Irish-born in the country in 1910, and their children amounted to 3,100,000 more. But there is no reliable way of assessing the number of third- or fourth-generation groups which then constituted a substantial portion of the whole, since all would have given English as their mother tongue to those who took the census of 1910.

organizations. But where numbers were large enough, points
of religious, linguistic, and cultural differences encouraged
the emergence of separate communities. In Michigan, Iowa,
New York, and North Dakota there were thriving communities of Hollanders; about 300,000 gave Dutch as their
mother tongue in 1910, a majority of them native American
children of immigrants. In the mining, mill, lumber, and
fishing towns of Massachusetts, Michigan, Wisconsin, Pennsylvania, and Washington, two hundred thousand Finnish-
Americans maintained their own identity. Of the three hundred thousand Americans of Swiss birth or parentage, those
who lived and worked together, as in the vineyards of
California or the restaurants of New York, were more likely
to stress their separate nationality than to slip in among the
Italians and Germans. The presence in the United States of
descendants of older immigrants with whom newcomers
identified themselves conditioned the adjustment of these
groups, as it had that of the Germans, the Irish, and the
Scandinavians.

The influences that played on the six hundred thousand
British subjects, other than the Irish, who made the crossing
in the ten years after 1900 were far more complicated. Obvi-
ously, they too had predecessors, perhaps two million of them
still living that year — with their children, not far from five
million. These immigrants had come from a variety of sources,
mostly in the last three decades of the nineteenth century.
Agricultural laborers and farmers from England, Scotland,
and Canada felt the lack of room at home and the attractiveness of opportunities in the New World. Operatives from the
textile mills, the potteries, and the steel and metal works of
England, and men out of the mines of Cornwall and Wales
brought over their skill and experience when employment was
slack in the Old Country or the wage differential high in the
new.

These people were foreign-born and felt some of the needs

of other immigrants. They celebrated accustomed holidays in the familiar way, drew together in fraternal orders and in charitable societies, established their own churches and newspapers. The Welsh, often bilingual, were nevertheless eager to preserve their language, and Scots and Cornishmen the distinctiveness of their dialects.

Yet these folk found it more difficult to define their own group. In the United States, the newly arriving British subjects encountered the American descendants of the earlier migrants of the seventeenth and eighteenth century. Similarity of language, religion, and manners brought them together; and the fact that the high level of skills enabled the English newcomers to take good places in industry and live well quickened the contact. The native-born and the newcomers could sometimes become communicants of each other's churches, readers of each other's newspapers, and members of each other's lodges. Episcopal churches and orders like the Odd Fellows and Foresters, originally set up by immigrants, thus lost their early character within a few decades.

Although these people did not feel the fears of other immigrants — that their children would not speak the ancestral language or that their religion might be lost — they nevertheless continued to identify themselves as British. That was due in part to an awareness of nationality they had brought with them and in part to the circumstances of settlement in the New World.

In the mill and mining towns, the English mechanics had an incentive to keep themselves separate from the Slovak or Hunky or Italian peasants. In the tin works, the potteries, the cotton and woolen mills, there was a premium on the skills of Welshmen or Staffordshiremen or Paisleymen or Yorkshiremen that induced them to flaunt their nativity as a sign of superior status. Everywhere attacks upon England by Irishmen drew together the loyal subjects of the Crown in defense of the land of their birth. Eager to pool their strength toward that end, they formed the British-American Association in 1895.

English birth was also a means of achieving an alliance with influential sectors of native society. These immigrants stressed their common Protestantism as against the unfamiliar religions of the other foreign-born. Thus Canadians and other British Orangemen supplied the nucleus shortly before the turn of the century for the American Protective Association (A.P.A.) which drew together all anti-Catholics. On this basis, many Irish Protestants counted themselves British while many English and Scottish Catholics of Irish ancestry fell in with the Irish-Americans. More generally, the growing interest in the Anglo-Saxon origins of the civilization of the United States encouraged the British to emphasize their group identity as evidence of their acceptability in American society. The way toward a sense of belonging seemed to lie in separateness rather than in undifferentiated assimilation.

There was no inconsistency in the fact. In the same years, the majority of Americans whose families had long been resident in the country were also seeking to separate themselves from the mass of their more recent fellow citizens. In the past, the ceaseless mobility with which this people had subjected their continent had not inclined them to any prolonged consideration of men's antecedents. But in their present world, so much occupied with Franco-Americans, Italian-Americans, German-Americans, and Irish-Americans, they could not escape the question, what manner of Americans they themselves were. And that question would be particularly pressing for those who had for some time come to rest, who had had the opportunity to strike roots.

In 1900, it was possession of a colonial past that was the symbol of belonging. Pride in the founders of the nation stimulated by the series of centennial celebrations put a high premium on eighteenth-century antecedents, and every American group labored to establish such antecedents for itself. For more

than a decade these interests had been expressed in the creation
of societies with ancestral membership qualifications. The un-
fortunates with no forebears to earn them admission to the
Sons of the American Revolution gained a vicarious sense of
participation by revealing the prominence in the colonies of
members of their own groups. Already the Germans, the
Irish, and the Jews, among others, had set up historical societies to make public their contributions to the early development of the country. The Italians, the Spaniards, and the Jews
were laying claims to Columbus; and the Irish and Scandinavians had uncovered compatriots who had made the New
World theirs before 1492. The quest for an American heredity
challenged the assumption that the early past of the nation was
entirely English; but implicitly it recognized the importance
of having such a past.

Under these circumstances, the groups which did enjoy the
distinction of descent from English colonists cherished it. Such
antecedents had long been a matter of pride to New Englanders. Early in the nineteenth century Timothy Dwight had
pointed to the relative freedom of his section from the incur-
sions of foreigners and had ascribed the distinctiveness of the
Yankee character to that freedom. The great migrations of
the last half of the century had brought to the region substantial groups of Irish and French-Canadians, Italians, Portuguese,
and Poles. But these newcomers stood largely apart from the
original inhabitants.

Though no longer a majority, Yankees were still a substantial element in the population of the section. The stubborn
countryside character who held on to the ancestral acres his
forebears had fought and conquered was the archetype of the
group, easily recognized in the novels of Mary Wilkins Freeman and Sarah Orne Jewett. Yet in actuality such people were
more often to be found in the cities than on farms. Newer
residents had relieved the Yankees of the burdens of industrial
labor. Typically, the New Englanders had risen into the pro-

fessions and into managerial or clerical positions, to which
education, character references, and family connections gave
them entree. As the immigrants preëmpted the central areas of
the cities, the older stock moved out toward the peripheral
suburbs, where it maintained the image of an older way of life
through town meetings and kept control of local politics,
schools, and other institutions.

By now these New Englanders felt fixed. In 1910, the census reported almost 90 per cent of those native to the section
still lived there. But it had not always been so. A century
earlier the most vigorous spirits of the region were deserting it,
abandoning the rocky farms of Massachusetts and Connecti-
cut to break the more fertile soil of the West. Through New
York, northern Ohio, Illinois, Kansas, and Iowa, these emigrants had stretched a band of settlement with ties to New
England. At the same time a Yankee commercial element had
been prominent in the developing cities of the middle states
and the Middle West and still retained a consciousness of its
origins.

In the outlands, the Yankees had been strangers, eager to
preserve their identity and the recollection of their place of
birth. Like other immigrants they had carried their churches
with them and had joined in benevolent societies to provide
entertainment for the fortunate and charity for the unfortunate. Congregational churches and New England societies
marked their progress across the nation. Generally they had
been able to impose a Yankee pattern upon the regions in
which they settled through the habits of communal oversight
and discipline inherited from the town. In some places, they
succeeded through their skill in dealing with the environment,
elsewhere through the capital and commercial connections
they brought with them, and still elsewhere through the constant recruitment from back home of editors, teachers, and
ministers who spread their ideas from press, pulpit, and desk.
In most areas the Republican Party was their instrument and

often they were wrapped up in the struggle for prohibition. They maintained links with New England by sending their children back to college, by the importation of books and magazines, and by membership in the Mayflower Descendants and kindred organizations.

British descent was also one of the marks of the Southerner. The great waves of nineteenth-century immigration had largely passed his section by; few new people had gone south of the Mason-Dixon line and those, by their fewness, were easily absorbed. In 1900, then, although men knew the Old South was dead and although some were already disillusioned with the new, it was possible to think of an identity of heritage that went back to Jamestown. The horizon now showed the factory stacks of Birmingham and Atlanta, but the region was still largely agricultural and its residents still largely lived by the soil.

The bulk of this population had always been yeomen. Out from this class of independent husbandmen had come, from time to time, individuals who comprised the planting aristocracy of Charleston or of tidewater Virginia or the black belt, or the mercantile elite of New Orleans and Richmond, or, now, the industrialists of Atlanta. But the inherited ideals still vigorous in the present came from an agrarian history.

The condition of the Southern farmer varied from place to place and had fluctuated markedly through the past. But everywhere it had been characterized by settlement that was dispersed, disorganized, and altogether individual. The family was the only cohesive social unit, its uniqueness reflected in a strong sense of cousinship. With each family an isolated entity, not subject to the controls of town or village, looseness of forms encouraged day-to-day hedonism. Men were often on the threshold of violence and found themselves frequently drawn to the relief of emotionalism; they were indulgent in the use of liquor and in sexual habits, and were attracted by enthusiasms in politics and religion.

Common British ancestry Southerners took for granted; often they pleased themselves with the romantic recollection of gallant English Cavalier or staunch Scottish Covenanter ancestors. They knew, of course, there had been Huguenots, Jews, and Germans in their past. But they assumed all had been absorbed into the prevailing English stock. The importance of color in their lives buttressed that assumption. Since all those on the black side of that decisive line were of one breed, it followed that all on the white side were too.

The Southerners had also long been on the move. From the Atlantic seaboard they had spread westward across the Mississippi to the states that had ultimately held to slavery and had joined the Confederacy. They had moved as well across the Ohio River into the lower sections of Ohio, Indiana, and Illinois, and on to California. In these places they retained their characters and beliefs and for a time continued to be known as Southerners. But outside their native region they found it difficult to maintain their identity as well as had the Yankees. They lacked the cohesive organs of social discipline, church, school, town. More important, so much of their unity rested on the contrast of black and white that they found it natural to mingle loosely with other whites of the most diverse antecedents.

For these people were not frozen within an old affiliation. Like the peasants from Austria who had become Poles and Slovaks, they and other Americans born in other parts of the country were in process of defining their identity. "The citizens from the shores of New England, from Ireland and Scotland, and from Germany form their societies in the state of New York"; why should not the "Ohio people" also do so? asked General Uronias Ewing. By contrast with the other groups about them, such Americans would think of themselves as "natives" or English or English-speaking. But there was nothing rigid about these groups. So long as they were voluntary in nature, they would continue to change in composition and in character as their members continued to adjust inherited cultures to the demands of new situations.[2]

Few groups could resist those changes, for to do so meant to cut their members off from the main currents of American life. The Pennsylvania Amish did so, and the Acadians of Louisiana, the secretarians in Amana and in other communal settlements. Perhaps the same might be said of such tightly-knit groups as the Boston Brahmins, the Knickerbocker Dutch, and the Philadelphia Quakers. But such stability was achieved only through social and spatial isolation that prevented contacts with outsiders.

More generally, the expansive conditions that prevailed in the United States brought together in their labor, their schooling, their government, their religion, and their marriage, individuals from diverse ethnic groups and prevented such isolation. Those encounters often produced strain, and sometimes conflict. But, for Americans whose affiliations were voluntary rather than dictated by color, those strains and conflicts could be resolved. And in resolution, they furthered the adaptation to American conditions of the patterns of life that some ancestor, immediate or remote, had brought to the New World from across some border.

CHAPTER IV

The Strains of a Free Society

The great migrations to the shores of the United States and within it had thrown together a variety of peoples. In a free society, they had been able to build the institutional and social life they desired. Affiliations formed in the process of settlement had defined diverse ethnic groups as those who recognized common antecedents held together. But Poles and Italians and Yankees did not in consequence live sealed off from one another. The same freedom that permitted them to draw off in some matters compelled them to have close contact with strangers. Such relationships, often strained and occasionally marked by bitter conflict, significantly influenced the role of these groups in the whole society.

The American economy centered on the individual. Each farm stood a functioning unit apart, each laborer occupied his own line on the payroll, each businessman was an account of the books of those with whom he traded. Dealing with each other in the anonymous terms of an impersonal market, Americans assumed that the cheapest seller always got the order, the most efficient worker the job, and the highest bidder the goods.

There were limits to that assumption however. In the realm of unskilled labor which almost all immigrants entered, to begin with at least, not all hands had equal access to employment. Faced with a multitude of men willing to work for the same low rate, contractors hiring a gang for construction or harvesting, or foremen adding to the staff of the factory might make their choice out of pure caprice. But they were more likely to take on those whom previous experience had proven satisfactory; in one place Negroes were reputed the good workers, in another Mexicans or Japanese. Or the employers were likely to select someone's cousins or friends, those who spoke a common language who would fit easily and docilely with the rest of the workers. In the smaller plants and sweat-shops the more intimate relationships of the hands with each other and with the boss put a premium on similarity. In many places, therefore, whole categories of labor were preëmpted by single ethnic groups: the Italians were the street laborers, the Greeks the shoeshine men, the Slovaks tended the steel mills. If an occasional stray drifted in, he was likely to be identified with the predominant group; in the Pennsylvania anthracite fields, Italians generally were known as Slavs.

Such preferences were more decisive above the lowest level of employment. In tasks that involved skills acquired through education or previous training and in callings that required capital or credit, some groups stood at an advantage. The miners or spinners with experience from Wales and England were likely to take the top jobs in Pennsylvania and Fall Riv-er. Jews who had sold ribbons and combs to the Polish peasants in Galicia were likely to find acquaintances to advance them the stock with which they could continue to do so in Chicago. Nor was it surprising that Armenians should hold practically a monopoly of rug peddling or that a Yankee lad with a high school diploma should find relatively easy access to employ-ment in banking and commerce.

Although the development of American production in these years dictated that industry should absorb an ever larger per-centage of manpower, and although newcomers always gravi-tated toward the lowest levels of employment, ethnic associa-tions largely determined the means by which individuals found their particular niches. This influence injected an element of stratification into the economic structure of the United States. Each group by its antecedents and by the nature of its settlement concentrated in certain employments, and that very concentration contributed to the awareness of its identity.

But those concentrations were not permanent. It was not usual that a son should follow his father's calling. A fluid and rapidly changing economy kept shifting the bases upon which possession of fortunes or entrenchment in crafts rested; and neither law nor custom recognized any means by which old priorities could be protected.

With every phase of the productive system expanding, outsiders were continually pushing in. The newcomers had always the attraction of willingness to work at minimal wages in order to get established and their pressure was difficult to resist. So the Irish who had manned the New England textile mills inexorably gave way to the more recent immigrants; Italians, Portuguese, Armenians, and French-Canadians edged in as pickers and sweepers, and soon were everywhere in the plant. Furthermore, sudden technological change repeatedly cut the ground from under once favored groups. The mechanization of coal mining and the replacement of less efficient processes by Bessemer furnaces thus enabled untrained Poles, Slovaks, and Italians to take the places of experienced Britishers. Finally, the spread of education enabled the sons of laborers to compete for situations with the sons of men higher in the occupational scale; the schools distributed the command of language, the practical skills, and the wish to push upward. All these factors lessened the importance of inherited advantages.

Groups already established resisted the encroachments of newcomers. It was hard, having struggled for years to secure the beginnings of better wages, to see the long lines of outsiders coming to the employer's assistance. Resentful measures of retaliation, under such conditions, sought to limit the endless competition. So in Fall River, the Irish operatives desecrated the rectory of the Catholic priest who had befriended the French-Canadian strikebreakers taking their jobs.

Trade unions became the established vehicles for expression of that resentment. The general humanitarian tradition of the labor movement induced men like Dan Tobin of the teamsters to argue Negroes ought to find a welcome in his trade and in his union; and the internationalism of the socialists found any barriers of race or nationality repugnant. Back in 1890, the American Federation of Labor had taken a stand against the color bar. But there was also a nativist tradition in the movement that had in the past involved it in Know-Nothing and anti-Oriental agitation and that would now lead it into a maze of restrictive practices.

The structure of the American Federation of Labor and of the independent railroad and printing crafts which acquired preëminence in this period encouraged stratification. Stressing pure and simple business unionism, the leaders rising to power regarded the internationalism of the socialists and, often, the whole humanitarian reform impulse as vague and impractical sentimentality. The outsider was a menace to their standards; they would keep him out. In membership and in procedures, these unions were not far different from ethnic Orders with benevolent and fraternal ends; and their rules and activities were sometimes enough to exclude strangers. The unions of garment workers were after all unions of Jews, just as the teamsters and carpenters were Irish, and the miners, British; they might have minorities of Italians, Yankees, or Slovaks, but those unacquainted with the language or habits of the majority were not likely to feel or to be welcome. Finally rules of apprenticeship, restrictions on numbers, and seniority provisions always gave the advantage to a closed circle of insiders. It was hardly necessary to set down explicit bans, as some unions did, to membership by colored or foreign-born workers.

But only in limited sectors of American industry were the unionized crafts able to hold their favored position. Elsewhere, mechanization progressively opened up ever more places for the unskilled who, in the great mass units of production, remained unorganized and outside the regulation as well as the protection of the labor movement.

Although the professions were still relatively open until 1914, they already showed signs of the influence of ethnic preferences. The ancient systems of apprenticeship through which young men had once entered these callings had disappeared. The schools which now offered the requisite training were open to all comers. These occupations, high in respectability and relatively high in income, were particularly attractive to the children of immigrants.

The sudden growth in numbers of doctors and lawyers and engineers produced the earliest hints of restriction through licensing. In medicine there was a gradual contraction of opportunities as the number of graduates fell from 5,204 in 1900 to 4,440 in 1910 and to 3,500 in 1915. Most important, success in practice often depended upon the favor of employers. Engineers without a connection to a firm or doctors not on a hospital staff were under a marked disadvantage; and in these forms of employment as in business there was an onus on certain identifications and a premium on others. Yankees and natives were on one level; Jews and Italians on another; and Negroes on still another. Among some groups, the creation of separate — Jewish, Swedish, Negro, or Catholic — hospitals compensated; and occasionally to be known as a Polish, Czech, or German doctor was an aid among an immigrant clientele, even when it was the same individual who thus variously described himself in the Polish, Czech, and German press. For the rest, the effort at establishment in the professions put an incentive upon shedding the tokens of unfavorable affiliations; to be a doctor meant to act, to talk, to look like the image of one. For all but those to whom color was a bar, that was possible, though the strain might take an emotional toll.

Yet, despite the evidences of strain, great areas of the economy were still free of barriers. Some callings, such as those in the theater or in sports, were almost entirely so; there talent was absolute. Elsewhere, as in construction, expansion was so rapid there were kinds of openings for all; if union tactics kept Negro and Jewish carpenters and painters off the new buildings, there was plenty of work on the old. And finally the strokes of fortune, of ingenuity, of skill, of venturesomeness were still capable of bringing sizable rewards to outsiders in business. The few who actually gained the golden prizes of success in commerce and industry were important beyond any counting of numbers for that success brought them leadership within their groups.

It was the same with the other means through which the groups maintained their separateness. Churches, societies, schools, and newspapers had helped define the lines that set one off from another; but individual members remained free, able, if they wished, in a fluid society to establish a variety of contacts which might in turn modify the nature of the group itself.

In American religious life the onus of choice remained individual. Many denominations stressed conversion as a process essential to the salvation of all their communicants. There were no legally recognized restraints and few socially sanctioned ones that held a member to the church of his fathers if he wished to leave it. The prevailing latitudinarianism, the belief that any church was good if it encouraged its members to lead a good life, induced considerable passing from one denomination to another. The difficulty of setting up new churches in new places sometimes pushed stray strangers into those already established. Missionary activities encouraged others to change their faith and men who broke the economic and social ties with their ancestral group often abandoned also its religious life.

The ethnic character of all denominations set limits to this movement. Catholics could not forget the bitterness that had only recently arrayed Yankee and British Protestants against them in the A.P.A. On the other hand, outsiders attracted intellectually or emotionally to Catholicism sometimes found it difficult to face the loss of social status conversion entailed and compromised with various forms of Anglo-Catholicism. But within these limits there was some passing.

More important, subtle pressure from the new environment Americanized the old churches. With none established, and all subject to the same conditions, there were the beginnings of striking changes. The French-Canadians would not think of ceasing to celebrate St. Jean Baptiste's day; but it seemed in time reasonable to move it from June 24 to July 4, to combine the patriotic and religious occasions. The gradual intrusion of English into the immigrant forms of worship and the beginnings of the transformation of the European priest into an American minister were evidences of the same force.

Finally, few ethnic groups pursuing their own separateness could avoid contact with strange coreligionists. The long series of conflicts among French-Canadian, Irish, native, and Italian Catholics were signs of the strain such contacts evoked. But there were other occasions when such folk, isolated, found the church a familiar refuge though it be in the hands of foreigners. Across the bounds of language and antecedents it was still possible to share the Mass. Ultimately, Catholics, like Lutherans and Jews, achieved workable compromises which gave communicants of every group the opportunity for identification they desired. Churchgoers thus had a choice of affiliations and the churches ineluctibly adapted themselves to their communicants' freedom to belong or not to belong.

The ethnic benevolent societies felt the same pressures. They held as members only those who wanted to be; each man had also the ability to be an Elk or Redman or, for that matter, to buy industrial insurance from a commercial company. That mobility, important to the individual because it enabled him to sever ties that no longer bound, also influenced the societies, for it tended to draw them into larger, more impressive and efficient units. Some lodges would gather into national ethnic federations. But they might also draw into larger religious groupings that appeared in the last quarter of the nineteenth century — the Catholic Foresters of America, the Catholic Knights of America, the Catholic Mutual Benevolent Association, and the Knights of Columbus, for instance. Or some might enter as branches into some wider order of Masons or Odd Fellows. Indeed it was well possible for individuals by multiple memberships to act in a variety of capacities and wear a variety of regalia.

Those who learned in the United States to take an Italian newspaper or to go to the Yiddish theater were also potential readers and audiences for the popular press and vaudeville. Intermediaries like Pulitzer and Hearst who catered to the tastes of the newcomers stimulated the trend, and the consistent spread of the common language facilitated it. Though the ethnic journals long survived and indeed grew in strength and continued to represent the particular tastes and attitudes of the group, the interest in the wider media reflected a growing awareness of the more general concerns of the world in which all lived together.

In politics, the newly arrived had often discovered their predecessors so well entrenched, with organizations so rigid as to preclude any accommodation. In New England, for example, the Irish who by now had with great difficulty gained power through the Democratic Party were not inclined to share it, and drove the French-Canadians and Italians into an alliance with the Yankees of the Republican Party.

But more often the necessities of politics forestalled the effort at aloofness. Machines, territorially organized, collapsed if they failed to adjust as the drift of population altered the character of neighborhoods. Martin Lomasney found it wise to conciliate the Jews who replaced the Irish residents of the West End of Boston; and Charles Murphy, Sachem of Tammany Hall, adopted a triumvirate of advisers, an Irishman, a Jew, and a German, reflecting in his choices the constituency he governed.

The fluidity of the economy, of religious and associational life, and of politics established contacts among individuals across the group lines they inherited. The free conditions of American society that permitted the ethnic entity voluntarily to take its form tested its vitality by keeping open to its members the possibility of withdrawal.

Therein the situation of the Negro and Oriental differed. Although at many points the adjustment of these people ran parallel to that of other ethnic groups, there was a critical difference: the act of adherence in the case of those marked by color was not altogether voluntary but was imposed from without.

The test of the difference was in the upbringing of the children. For it was through the children that the sense of ethnic identity passed from generation to generation. Most boys and girls felt the pressures toward change even more acutely than had their parents; the children could move from the neighborhood, the job, the lodge, the church of their fathers. In addition, compulsory education to which all were subjected drew them together. Some, necessarily, through parental insistence stood apart in parochial institutions. But most passed for some time through the public schools; and even if there, or in afternoon classes, they learned the old folks' language, they had still the opportunity to meet other young people, be familiar with other values of other cultures. Choices opened constantly before them. It might be no more than a change of name — from Roy to King or Schwartz to Black — or it might involve a more fundamental shift of loyalties, but the ability to decide was evidence of control over their own affiliations.

Although mostly they married within the ethnic groups — for it was thus acquaintanceships were made and friendships struck — there was still considerable intermarriage. In the

American ideal, marriage was a free union between isolated individuals swayed by romantic love and disregardful of external barriers. There were efforts to limit such selections. On the part of the parents of course. In the tight upper ranks of Eastern seaboard cities, among the Boston Brahmins, or in Main Line Philadelphia, the control of inherited fortunes or the threat of exclusion from society might serve that end. Religious pressures operated in the same direction. Frightened by the trend, the Catholic Church in 1907 made its rules more stringent, as did a series of pronouncements by Jewish rabbis at about the same time. But even the marriage of an Italian with an Irish Catholic, of a Polish with a German Jew involved a break with ethnic ties. In any case, neither law nor custom recognized these distinctions, and the ultimate decision was individual.

The contrast with the situation of colored people was striking. The extent of intermarriage was slight. As with other ethnic groups, the separateness of religious and social institutions encouraged young men and women to seek partners of their own kind. But in addition, the law in many states declared mixed marriages illegal and nowhere were there significant expressions of the opinion that racial fusion might be desirable.

Consequently the Negroes, unlike the whites, could not have multiple affiliations. The offspring of a union between a German and an Irishwoman might preserve through life ties with the ethnic groups of both his parents. But the colored man, no matter what the elements in his actual heredity, in the eyes of society and of the law, was all black. The involuntary and total character of the color line to that extent distinctively set him apart from the rest of the population. He therefore remained a jarring exception to the pattern by which others adjusted the forms of their lives to their needs through the contacts of the free society of the United States.

The strains of economic, religious, social, and family adjustment as ethnic groups encountered each other were familiar from the distant past. This was simply the most turbulent manifestation of the existence of such groups, a characteristic of their society taken for granted by almost all Americans. That the United States was a conglomeration of many diverse elements was also taken for granted.

The American scene was popularly pictured as a remarkably active and variegated place. Through it wandered a host of dissimilar figures reflecting the variety of origins and affiliations of real life. In the novels, magazines, and newspapers of wide circulation and on the vaudeville stages, these figures appeared as a matter of course, represented by conventional stereotypes which embodied the commonly accepted images of each group. The Yankee, the Irishman, the German, the Englishman, the Jew, the Negro were each completely recognizable by the characteristics it was presumed they held in common. The crude characterizations often involved general judgments: the frugal Yankee, the drunken Irishman, the sentimental German, the condescending Englishman, the grasping Jew, the shiftless Negro. But whatever their accuracy or justice, these characterizations did not deny to each group its place in the total life of the nation.

For the heterogeneity of population, so sharply at variance with the situation in every other part of the world, Americans had a traditional explanation. What set them off from other peoples was precisely diversity of origins. This was a young nation, always expanding and always involved in a continuing process of settlement. There was therefore room for representatives of all the tribes of the Old World.

Not only was America a new land; Americans were a new people. Their character was not yet fixed. Descended from Europeans, they would yet be unlike any of their ancestors, for their qualities would be determined by the free environment in which they lived. The addition of new strains was not repugnant to new men who, indeed, welcomed any fresh traits that might contribute energy and variety to the evolving national type. The United States was a melting pot which absorbed every difference of temperament and character and from which would emerge an ultimate product stronger than any of its constituent elements. The throngs in Washington, Chicago, and New York, who came to cheer Zangwill's play, *The Melting Pot*, were moved by recognition of an ancient American dream. "The play succeeded with the people" because it was "a play of the people," and contained "the national vision" within which America was "creating the future race by blending all races."[1]

Only a few Americans in 1900 questioned that long-held assumption. But the questions they raised would come to intrude ever more prominently in the consciousness of their fellow citizens and before long would raise annoying doubts as to the validity of the old idea. Did the melting pot actually make Americans out of the motley host that had crowded into the Republic? Did the newcomers actually strengthen the fabric of its social life?

For some who raised the questions, the evidence was alarming. The most pressing problems with which industrialization and urbanization had endowed the nation seemed ever to implicate the immigrants. The teeming slums of the great new cities, dark in the dirt of their unsanitary tenements, were altogether strange and unprecedented to the American landscape; but then, language and appearance identified the denizens of these unwholesome places as Italians or Jews. Scandal besmirched the officeholders; the ballot box, corrupted, no longer recorded the voice of the people; and the law, contemned, exercised no restraint over criminals; but then, the names in the newspapers were German and Irish. It was the same with intemperance or illiteracy or the low level of wages; at the root of every difficulty were, if not the Poles, then the French-Canadians, or Greeks, or some other outlandish folk.

An earlier America presumably had not known these evils. Manifestly, the argument was, they were habits imported by

the foreigners. Since these conditions were not native to the
New World, it was unthinkable that they be allowed to persist; the ignorant and poor must be induced to alter their alien
ways of life, to pull themselves out of the filth and corruption
in which they wallowed and to become like their more fortunate fellow citizens, Americanized. Certainly there was an
obligation that these people live in the houses, behave in the
patterns, dress in the clothes, and talk in the accents, becoming
to Americans.

In such demands were two hidden assumptions of great
significance. The injunction that the newcomers must conform to an American style of life took for granted that such a
style of life with a distinctive American character actually
existed. The attempts to define that Americanism most often
drifted away in the nostalgic pretense that the great hostile
cities were not there, that the rural past still was real, and that
the old virtues of self-reliance, independence, thrift, venturesomeness, could be found in the whole population. Perhaps it
was because they themselves bore so little resemblance to this
image of America, that many Americans insisted on ascribing
the blame to the Outsiders, insisted on hoping that if only
those others conformed, all might revert to a purer, pleasanter
state.

The injunction that the most recent comers slough off all the
traits of their dissimilarity also implied that homogeneity was
itself socially desirable. For the clear corollary was that uniformity was "the basis of healthy national life"; the population
had to "be homogeneous to such a point that the minority"
would be "willing to accept the decision of the majority on
all questions." "To be cosmopolitan," the Boston Transcript
pointed out, was "to be badly governed."[2]

Resentment against the immigrant spilled over to stain even
the children and grandchildren of earlier immigrants. Born in
the country, these Americans nevertheless retained some loyalties and affiliations with roots overseas. Here and there the

ethnic group was criticized, beaten with the ugly word hyphenism. Thinking enviously of the "unity of sentiment" in
France, Germany, and England, E. A. Ross thus warned that
the United States in a national crisis would be sorely torn by
"internal confusion, dissension and cross-purposes."[3]

These suspicions were most often voiced by New Englanders, at home or removed to the Middle West. There were indications in plenty that Yankees were no longer playing the
role they once had in the affairs of the nation. The halls of
Congress which had once echoed to the oratory of Webster
and Adams now were unruffled by the frigid maneuverings of
Aldrich and Lodge; such was the measure of the decline. Even
in state and local politics the descendants of the Puritans were
driven to an uneasy sharing of control. By the same token there
were everywhere threats to their ascendancy in the public
schools, to their stability in the old churches. Economically
the section lagged behind other parts of the country. The men
of great wealth were still of Yankee antecedents; but they
were finding themselves in uncomfortable proximity to a
crowd of outrageously prosperous newcomers, without status,
without respectable family ties, without proper sense of social
responsibility. Among the spokesmen of the group there was
much show of contempt for the plutocracy although curious-
ly the primary butts of their dislike were the unenviable mob,
who, after all, were more vulnerable to ridicule than the new
nobility of oil and steel.

Why had the former dominance slipped away? The mere
power of numbers had thrust the old stock into a helpless
minority. Weakened during the Civil War, they liked to point
out, by sacrifices of manpower in the cause of the Union, a
falling birth rate ever since had sapped the Yankee strength.
And what had caused the declining fecundity of which statistical studies and the very appearance of the streets gave
evidence? Why, the thronging newcomers had so depressed
the standard of living that people of intelligence, virtue, fore-

sight, and self-control limited the size of their families while
the ignorant and shiftless, caring only for the passionate pleasures of the moment, bred to their heart's content.

The Brahmin leadership of the New England group felt the
sense of loss most acutely. The distressing contrast between
their own inadequacy and the competence of their immediate
forebears drove the young men who had matured in New
England in the 1880's and 1890's into a relentless drive to emphasize their ancestry. As if to set themselves off in terms of
antecedents, they embarked upon a thoroughgoing rediscov-
ery of their Englishness — in religion, in education, in politics,
in style of life. At the end of the journey was the revelation of
the Anglo-Saxon origins of their culture. As Henry Cabot
Lodge once put it, the English alone of the people of Europe
were "a race almost entirely fixed" in character.[4] They had
created the United States and now seemed doomed to share
the fate of the buffalo.

The prospect of permanent caste lines in America or of a
dread race war was unthinkable. In the inheritance of the
Adamses and Quincys and Lodges was a whole body of democratic ideas which they could not reject without doing violence to filial feelings. That was their dilemma.

The young men who established the Immigration Restriction League in 1894 saw one way out. Halt the flow of newcomers and allow the mass irrevocably here to settle down.
Then the pressure of the superior abilities and natural leadership of the Yankees would assert itself and mold the aliens in
an American form. The appropriate device for achieving the
desired exclusion was a literacy test. The bulk of inferior Europeans would be held back while a sprinkling of exceptional,
picturesque individuals would be admitted, but in numbers
too small to create serious problems.

The Immigration Restriction League attracted gratifying
academic support. Scholars, convinced that social data could
be organized into a science applicable to questions of current

policy, had long been struggling, with only moderate success, to correct the political and economic disorders of the nation. Regulation of immigration offered an opportunity, on a vast scale, for social engineering that would not disturb important vested interests. Economists and sociologists, who feared that the closing of the frontier had brought the era of expansion to an end, viewed with alarm the effects of the continued inpouring — the curtailment of opportunities, the growth of poverty, and the bitterness of class struggle. Restriction, like conservation, became an essential part of social planning. Only by limiting the right of entry to desirable newcomers, explained Henry Pratt Fairchild, would the "domination of capital" be curbed and the lower elements of society be pulled up out of their degradation.[5]

It was not hard to tell which were the desirable newcomers; the new biological and social sciences had the answers. From the work of the nineteenth-century European theorists of race, E. A. Ross and John R. Commons, among others, had taken over the concept of separate and unequal genera of mankind. From Darwinian speculations the social engineers had absorbed the notion of a struggle for survival among species. And from Galton and the eugenicists they had acquired the idea that they could control hereditary traits by the careful selection of stocks for breeding. In the atmosphere generated by the current debate over the Negro, over the Orientral, and over the implications of American imperialism, they had not far to go to reach the conclusion that fixed racial lines divided the various groups of Europeans from one another.

There was much experimentation in these years with categories that might separate the fit from the unfit. The reputable Anglo-Saxon was the nuclear element. But to practical men the tactical disadvantage of such narrow limits were clear. Teutonic or Anglo-Teutonic were terms that mobilized greater potential political support; but even those designations left

out the Irish, by now no mean body of voters. The restrictionists were drawn therefore to a simpler distinction between
the "old" and the "new" stocks. The former originated in the
northwest of Europe, and were desirable Aryan or Nordic
kinsmen of the original settlers. The latter originated in the
south and east and were Slavs, Mediterraneans, or Semites,
"beaten men of beaten races." [6]

The most substantial accession of support from which the
restrictionists profited in these years came from south of the
Mason-Dixon line. Immigration had not been a pressing problem in that region. Preoccupation with the Negro had made
all other divisions secondary. Indeed many whites at the opening of the century had looked with favor to the coming of any
Europeans as a means of reducing the dependence upon black
labor; and almost every state for a time had sponsored organized efforts to attract newcomers to its borders. The failure
of these campaigns was disappointing and the final blow when
the Supreme Court held them illegal turned many Southerners
against any continued immigration.

There was some support also from the ranks of organized
labor. The remnants of the Knights of Labor were bitter in
opposition to further immigration. The A. F. of L. had long
shown its dislike of the newcomers, had early drawn an anal-
ogy between exclusion of the Chinese and exclusion of other
competitors in the labor market. Although the presence in its
ranks of some immigrants and of many children of immigrants
prevented the Federation from taking a clear stand, it regu-
larly encouraged the proponents of restriction.

But such aid was still not enough. Prolonged agitation several times brought the anti-immigration forces to the verge of
success; each time some final obstacle intervened. The struggle
culminated in 1911 with release of the report of the Dillingham
Committee. With the connivance of President Roosevelt who
secretly sympathized with them, the restrictionists had gained
control of this committee, commissioned by Congress in 1907

to investigate the whole subject of immigration. Its labors produced a number of studies of considerable importance. But the summary report, often running counter to the evidence, was biased and furnished a basis for recommendation of the literacy test. When the bill failed to become law despite that support, the long restrictionist drive seemed to come to an unsuccessful close.

"To hell with Jews, Jesuits and steamships," wrote Prescott Hall when President Taft vetoed the literacy bill.[7] He expressed thus the accumulated resentments stored up in two decades of agitation. Indeed the only result of all that effort had been to stir up a brew of bitter animosities. The vague feelings of group hostility that emerged followed no consistent pattern. But the long debate had conjured up dark doubts as to who belonged in the United States and who did not. Under the pressure of those doubts troubled men turned against their fellows, as if by pushing away the alien others they could make themselves at home.

By the end of the period the old stereotypes were acquiring new and darker shadows. Anti-Catholicism, declining in vigor since the collapse of the A.P.A. in the 1890's, took a new lease on life as Tom Watson launched an offensive campaign against the Church in the South. Objections to the most recent immigrants added venom to the old antagonisms. The swarthy Italians, dubious as to color, were denied kinship to a glorious Roman or Renaissance past. Instead, they were set off in a separate species — South Italians, ignorant, violent, depressed, filthy, and, as the Virginia legislature put it, bound to "their Mafia and Black Hand murder societies."[8]

A new animus attached itself to the Jew. Tom Watson's hatred touched off the lynching in Georgia of young Frank on a trumped-up charge of murder and that ignited a chain of hostility that surrounded the Jews with suspicion; in each itinerant peddler was the specter of a Wall Street or international banker, in each laborer a potential revolutionary. The

barbarism imputed to the Slavs justified the harsh feelings directed against Poles and Slovaks just as cleverness made plausible the dislike of the insidious Syrians. The Mexicans increasingly felt the weight of the discrimination that already
bound the Negroes and Orientals.

All too often the readiest defense was to seek to align one-
self with the attackers against some less fortunate group. In the
turbulent agitation against the Chinese and Japanese, white
immigrants were long prominent. Syrians and Armenians
claimed a special immunity from criticism because they were,
they said, the Yankees of the Near East. An Italian editor
added to his own security by establishing a contrast with the
Jews. Which would be the more dangerous, he asked, "the
Russian Hebrew who goes peddling with his matches . . . or
the Italian peasant who goes to plant vineyards in California?" [9]

The evidences of strain heralded the ills of the future. For
the present, however, the consequences were held in check by
prevailing forces in American society. In most ethnic groups,
"old" as well as "new," the majority saw through the arguments of the restrictionists. The literacy test, the *Milwaukee
Journal* pointed out, "is but a plaster prescribed by nativist
doctors for the purpose of hiding sores . . . not caused by
immigration." What threatened Italians and Hungarians immediately, it added, would ultimately also threaten Germans
and Scandinavians.[10]

The struggle over immigration policy evoked eloquent jus-
tifications of the tradition of free entry as well as the violent
assaults upon it. The efforts to close the gates were defeated
not only because certain business interests wished the labor
supply to keep growing, and not only because sentimentalists
thought a sprinkling of exotic nationality lent "zest to life and
a picturesque interest to . . . cities." The restrictionists went
down because there was still vitality to the old belief in America as the land of new men. From the heart of Yankeedom,
President Eliot of Harvard University through these years

continued to defend the ideal of diversity and insisted that people separated in their groups could still "live together side by side in perfect peace and amity." [11]

That attitude was the legacy of a past in which fluidity and mobility, the products of ceaseless expansion, were constant. This society, in its freedom, had resilience enough to absorb the strains of its own rapid change and of the adjustment of the various groups within it to each other's presence.

WAR AND RESTRICTION

CHAPTER V

World War

Like the sudden August storms that burst unattended yet leave all changed behind them, the outbreak of war in Central Europe interrupted the course of American life. For three uneasy years the nation waited at the brink of involvement, suffered from the reflected tremors, then plunged itself into the conflict.

The impact of war had an immediate effect on the whole population of the country. Directly, the outbreak of fighting cut off the movement of people from Europe. The active attempt to blockade the continent and the persistent blows against Allied shipping made all transatlantic traffic dangerous and reduced the flow of newcomers to a trickle. In addition the barriers erected by the belligerent powers within the continent broke the whole chain of communications that had facilitated and stimulated immigration. In the years of the fighting, 1915–1919, only 530,000 newcomers entered the United States from Europe. The arrival of new people was for the time being, at least, not an effective element in the development of the American population. The results could be observed in the census of 1920. The 105,700,000 Americans of that year were 13,700,000 more numerous than a decade earlier. But their rate of increase was the lowest in their history.

The population already in the United States indirectly felt the war also. The closing down of the supply of new labor put additional strains on the agricultural and industrial systems, which were in any case being reshaped by the pressure of war and of war orders. The consequence was a marked movement of people within the continent, a series of internal migrations, the implications of which approached in importance the movements of the nineteenth century.

In the Southwest, the shortage of willing workers was chronic. Production of fruits and vegetables continued to grow in volume, and the steady extension into Arizona and southern California of the cultivation of long-staple cotton added grievously to the demand for pickers. Yet the anti-Oriental agitation had already closed off one obvious source of supply.

The eagerness to take on any drifter capable of relieving the seasonal pressures attracted a colorful army of toilers. By way of Hawaii came thousands of Portuguese, Spaniards, and Puerto Ricans, earlier recruited for labor in the sugar and pineapple plantations, but now aware of the greener pastures on the mainland. From a more distant possession came a substantial number of Filipinos. But the total of all these stray groups was inadequate to the demand.

The remedy was to add to the number of Mexicans, close at hand and easily drawn across the border. There had never been serious obstacles in the way of those who made this crossing; and it was simple to evade the few requirements such as the head tax. Illegal entries of this sort were already common and would continue so. But to stimulate the migration further, the Secretary of Labor on May 22, 1917, ordered immigration officials to disregard the most irksome restrictive provisions and to facilitate the admission of agricultural workers from Mexico. By 1920, the number of Mexican-born had almost doubled. Some pushed north to Colorado or even Michigan, but mostly they remained in the Southwest.

Elsewhere in the United States, farmers faced some of the same pressures, but met the crisis by stepping up the pace of mechanization and by increasing wages to hold the existing labor force. Therefore, outside the Southwest, the manpower problem was more likely to be of active concern to the manufacturing than to the agricultural entrepreneur. Cut off from the sources at which it had been accustomed to replenish its supply of labor, the crying need of industry was for a new flow of cheap hands. In desperation, employers turned to the regions where cheap labor was to be found. Through the South, agents and advertisements spread word of the well-paid opportunities in the North. But the high, and rising, rates of wages were the most effective recruiting agents of all.

Among the tenant farmers and sharecroppers, white and black, the response was impressive. But the reaction of the Negroes was particularly striking. Coming after the boll weevil epidemic of 1915 had depressed already low living standards, the tidings from the North were omens of salvation. To those who had handed on to them the glad news in the *Chicago Defender* that there were places "where a man is a man," and well-paid at that, movement out of the South became a glorious second emancipation. It was of a promised land, a Canaan, a flight out of Egypt, they sang, as they moved away on the crowded "club rate" cars provided by the railroads. By 1920, the colored population of New York had leaped by 66 per cent to 152,000, of Chicago by 148 per cent to 109,000, of Cleveland by 307 per cent to 34,000 and of Detroit by 611 per cent to 40,000. In scores of lesser towns the Negroes took places in mills and mines, occupied whole residential districts, and established communities that would continue to draw their fellows in succeeding decades.

This movement was part of a more general process of internal migration that involved both regional shifts and a drift to the cities, where were the opportunities of the new economic condition. In this period the South and the prairie states lost the capacity to hold their residents while the new industrial districts of the Middle West from Pittsburgh to

Chicago and the whole Pacific coast demonstrated the ability to attract newcomers. But the mobility of the era was more marked still; for within every section there was a simultaneous drift from the rural to the urban regions. By 1920 more than half the population lived in urban places, which in the decade had shown an increase of 38 per cent as contrasted with an increase of 10 per cent in rural places. In 1920 more than 27,000,000 people lived in the sixty-eight cities with populations of 100,000 or more.

The accelerated rate of mobility produced complex social repercussions. It complicated the earlier difficulties of moving — the loosening of family ties and the weakening of social discipline, the sense of insecurity and the loneliness that came from separations. Coming in the midst of the war, this movement involved additional adjustments. Those who came into the cities found wages higher; but they also found prices rising steadily, and decent housing so short as to be unobtainable. The impact was harder on those who, like the Negro, were not altogether free to choose in what districts they should live. But it was hard on all, left many for long intervals unsettled. At the same time, wartime prosperity encouraged self-indulgence in amusements and often a lowering of moral standards. Given the inadequacy of housing and the removal of the restraints that come from the exchange of the oversight of the small town for the anonymity of the city, the transition left men with the unhappy sense that they knew not where they were, nor with whom they belonged, nor what they wished to do with themselves.

The regions that lost population also felt the unsettling effects. In the South there were rumors of turpentine works shut down, of acres of sugar and rice gone to waste, because of hands who had fled. True or not, these stories reflected the panicky fear of being abandoned. The white man, indignant at the Negroes' flight, was the more indignant because it revealed the extent of his dependence upon their labor. The possibility that the blacks, for so many years proclaimed a burden to the South, might actually escape and leave it to confront all sorts of other difficult problems was terrifying and degrading. And in the efforts to hold the Negroes where they were were mingled blandishments and threats, promises of better treatment and dire predictions as to the consequences of disloyalty. It was as if the Southerners too saw in this cataclysmic shuffling of population the beginnings of a frightening new era.

In the context of these changes Americans approached the critical issues of ethnic affiliation raised by the war. Restrictionist agitation had already rendered every group sensitive to questions of its identity and of its relationship to other groups. The outbreak of fighting in Europe created perplexing problems, the solution of which vitally affected society in the United States. Yet those solutions were reached while large segments of the population were disturbed by the dislocations of the war years.

Even before 1917, while the United States was still a bystander, the question of participation had already aligned substantial factions in opposing camps which struggled to determine the course of national policy. The conflict that ensued brought to the fore questions of the nature of group loyalties that, until then, had largely been taken for granted.

President Wilson had at first asked the nation to remain neutral in thought as well as in action. By implication he had demanded that Americans suspend judgment as to the relative merits of the powers involved. But, almost at once, he was impatient with such impartiality and began to desert the ideal standard he had himself set. Despite his professions, he could not resist his own loyalties, his sense of kinship to Britain that sprang out of his education and out of his awareness of his own Scotch-Irish heritage. This consciousness had earlier exposed itself in his work as a historian. His writings had given form to the assumptions, prevalent among many Southerners and New Englanders, that the United States was still joined by genealogy and culture to the motherland, England.

Wilson was plagued not only by the inherent difficulties of his situation but also by the inability to recognize the scope of the problem. Neutrality could not be simply laid down as a policy by proclamation. From within the country and from outside it, powerful forces would come to bear upon the resolution of the issue.

The British government, determined to secure the participation of the United States, had at hand effective instruments for assuring it. There was no need in London to scurry about for devices hastily fashioned for the occasion. For two decades, Englishmen had increasingly become aware of the growing prominence of the United States and of the necessity for establishing ties across the Atlantic.

Practical considerations shaped that awareness. With the shift of the balance of power in Europe as Germany rose in strength and developed her navy, English statesmen began to fear for the security of the empire. In the emerging alignment of the great nations, the United States, now also a colonial power with global interests, was potentially the decisive ally and had to be won over.

An Anglo-American understanding was not only expedient, but in the ideology of British imperialism, justified. Contact with the backward people of the world had generated a kind of racialism among the administrators, conscious of the vast gulf between themselves and those they ruled. Confronted by a mass of barbaric humanity to be civilized and governed, many imperialists lacked confidence in their own endurance for the endless task. As the nineteenth century drew to a close, it seemed logical to turn for assistance to their blood brothers, to share their burdens with the overseas Anglo-Saxons. Benjamin Kidd thus appealed to the English-speaking people of the world to take up the common duty imposed on them by their superior heredity.

To that end it was important, as the Earl of Rosebery and Lord Cromer both recognized, to stress the racial unity of the Anglo-Saxons. Cecil Rhodes had planned a secret society of men of Nordic race trained to rule the world; his vague imperialistic dream in practice became a scholarship association that brought Americans, among others, to study in the English universities. But the prosaic outcome was more significant than the flamboyant dream. The successive groups of young men who passed through Oxford returned to the United States imbued with a sense of new loyalty to Old England. "They had felt at home at Oxford," a Maryland scholar recalled, "and English, Americans and Colonials were glad to come there as one family and one brotherhood." [1] Through the Atlantic Union and the English-Speaking Union, Englishmen labored to persuade their transatlantic cousins that an identity of interests united the quondam mother country with the lost colonies. The objective from the end of the nineteenth century onward was to achieve a coördination of foreign policy. Any tendency, even in purely domestic matters, was ominous if it threatened to draw the United States away from British affiliations. Many Englishmen, after 1900, were consequently convinced "that immigration must stop." The hordes of continentals who were diluting the Anglo-Saxon strain were to be excluded if America was to remain as she was.

The gathering tide of pro-English sentiment in the United States drew support from the large body of British immigrants in the New World. The influence of these newcomers was not simply a product of numbers. Relatively high in social and economic status, literate in the language of the country, English-, Welsh-, and Scottish-Americans were not as conspicuously strange as the other foreign-born. Among the English immigrants were some men in positions of leadership in American society — notably a large number of Episcopal clergy, such as William T. Manning, S. Parkes Cadman,

William Carter, G. A. Oldham, Walter Laidlaw, and C. A. Eaton, and a significant number of newspaper and magazine editors. These people bore none of the accepted signs of alien antecedents; sometimes their nativity was not commonly known. Those facts, which seemed to indicate they had no axe to grind, undoubtedly added to their influence.

Against this weighty sentiment in favor of the Allies were arrayed the most numerous immigrant ethnic groups. The German-Americans had already committed themselves to support of the imperial nationalism of Bismarck and the Kaiser. This commitment, established in the first decades after the creation of the empire, had been cemented by the high esteem in which German culture was held generally in the United States. German-Americans had no doubts as to the righteousness of the cause for which their fatherland fought; attacks upon Germany only strengthened the sense of loyalty to the land of their birth or antecedents. Confronted by the crisis of war, the German-American Alliance broadened the scope of its activities. Its usual cultural work seemed now less pressing than the immediate task of defending the Central Powers against the accusations of Allied propaganda; and personal and family ties accentuated the urgency of collecting funds for war relief.

A critical alliance with the Irish-Americans strengthened German-American opposition to involvement in the conflict on the side of France and England. In the long years of agitation for Irish Home Rule, the sons of Erin in the United States had nurtured a bitter sense of hostility toward the British. Well before the outbreak of hostilities, there had been efforts to establish a *rapprochement* between the Ancient Order of Hibernians and the German-American Alliance to influence domestic and foreign policy. After 1915 it was clear to many Irish nationalists that England was too powerful; she would never be made to yield, they thought, by parliamentary agitation. Gradually extremists like Jeremiah

O'Leary and John Devoy won over a large following. In March of 1916 some two thousand delegates at an Irish Race Convention were told, "In the outcome of the great war . . . we have one supreme interest . . . to see England, the tyrant and oppressor of Ireland . . . defeated." [2] That very year the Easter Rebellion demonstrated the weakness of an unaided insurrection and the futility of lingering hopes for Home Rule. The savage British repression antagonized even the moderate Irish-Americans. The conclusion was inescapable that independence could come only through the assistance of one of the Great Powers. The Irish-Americans were tempted to favor any nation likely to resist their traditional oppressor.

Local American frictions intensified this hostility to Britain. In New England, for instance, the British-Americans and Yankees had been closely involved in the anti-Catholicism of the A.P.A. (American Protective Association). In politics, in society, and in industry, these groups were often openly anti-Irish. Yet these were now the closest friends of England. That was in itself enough to keep Irish animosity alive.

For altogether different reasons, the Jews of America distrusted the Allies. Russia loomed largest in the consciousness of this group. For thirty years Jews had learned to regard the empire of the czars as the implacable enemy of their co-religionists. Since 1881, Russia had generated the most reactionary tendencies in the life of the old continent and had directed and supported anti-Semitic movements everywhere from France to Romania. Only ten years before the war, the outbreak of pogroms had aroused a storm of protest among Americans of every creed; and in 1913 the United States had broken off commercial relations with the czarist government in protest against regulations that discriminated against American citizens of the Jewish faith. Jews were therefore hardly disposed to regard with favor an alliance in which Russia was a prominent, some would have said the predominant, partner.

Germany, by contrast, was the shining symbol of the progressive improvement of the status of the Jews. Bismarck's empire had steadily liberalized its laws and had eliminated all political and civic restrictions based on religion. Although anti-Semitic agitators occasionally made themselves heard there, as throughout central Europe, their influence was slight and German Jews had risen to positions of considerable economic and social eminence. Above all, Germany had been the source of the enlightenment and of the emancipation that had brought Jews back into the life of the modern world. Germany was expected to provide in the future, as it had in the past, the cultural stimulus to continuing integration into American life.

The sympathizers with the Central Powers did not expect actively to help Germany and Austria. Control of the seas by the Allies isolated the Fatherland; and the evolving policy of the American government discouraged occasional efforts to contribute such assistance. It was plain that any aid extended by the United States, or by Americans, would aid the Allies. German sympathizers early realized their best course was to work for neutrality.

The neutrality position gained the support of several groups not linked to any belligerent nation and opposed to any participation in the war. American Scandinavians, both in imitation of the policy of their homelands and as a result of anti-militarist convictions, strongly favored a peace policy. A great inchoate trend of Middle-Western opinion, of which W. J. Bryan was spokesman, was pacifist by conviction and had been suspicious of all foreign ties since the agitation of the silver question in which they had come to think of gold as the tool of international bankers. These people felt no direct concern in the war; they wished to stay out of it; and they were therefore potential allies of the positive German sympathizers.

In the background of events were the confused wishes of

groups more recently settled in the United States, groups with political experience too brief to permit immediate formulation of opinions. Often loyalties were confused. Italians had been unhappy about military service, antipathetic to the state and to war; but they could not help identifying themselves with cousins and friends actually in service or fail to feel the shock and elation of victory and defeat. That confusion was confounded when, as in the case of the Poles, service was for foreign monarchs, Austrian, Prussian, or Russian, as the case might be. There was vaguely the wish that the disasters of war might not extend also to the New World; but there was also the consciousness that people such as they could do little to influence the course of events. And the overriding anxiety in each case was to conform to what America expected.

As the issues of the war became clearer, the nationalistic leaders within each group began to estimate the possibilities of profiting by its opportunities; and the European powers began to fish in these troubled waters. Russia proclaimed itself the defender of the Orthodox Slavs everywhere against their Teutonic and Magyar oppressors. On the other hand the Austrian and Hungarian governments called for the support of their overseas subjects. "Our sweet Hungarian fatherland is in danger," wrote Zoltán Kuthy; the men had gone off to fight, the women and children were in danger, financial aid was needed.[3] Gradually, the Albanians became pro-, and the Armenians anti-Turk. Italians from Sicily heard more of the distant unredeemed provinces in the hands of Austria. Polish hopes leaped for a united and independent state although how that might come about was unclear since powers on both sides held portions of the anticipated territory. Yet in 1917 all these nationalistic aspirations were still inchoate, and had little effect upon the evolution of American policy.

In April 1917, the United States entered the war. The decision was the product of a complex of political, economic, and cultural forces that persuaded Wilson that the defeat of Germany was in the American interest. In that decision the weight of ethnic loyalties was certainly strong, not least so in the case of the President himself.

Entry into the conflict disposed of the immediate issue of foreign policy and seemed at once to put an end to internal dissension. All Americans in practice buried the differences that had earlier separated them and drew unitedly into the war effort. In the recruitment of manpower, in the sale of war bonds, and in the general enlistment of energies in 1917 and 1918, the Americans of German or Irish descent who had been reluctant to become involved were no less prominent than those who had strongly urged a belligerent role upon the United States. Furthermore President Wilson, determined to direct the terrible necessities of war toward some good end, insisted upon phrasing its slogans, and ideals, in terms that had international humanitarian relevance. He emphasized the distinction between the German people and the German government and hoped thus to minimize the chauvinistic by-products of the fighting. The leaders of the Irish-American and German-American communities could conscientiously shift to the support of such aims and repress any tendencies "harmful to the unity so necessary here for the success of the war." [4]

Yet this wholehearted coöperation did not allay the feelings of hostility and bitterness stirred up earlier in the debate over neutrality. The very agitation of the question had accentuated the sense of nationalism among all groups. The views then exchanged would not readily be forgotten, and the heat of that argument would long generate resentment.

The confusion of voices in this discussion of so fateful a step in American foreign policy distressed those Americans anxious to have the nation assume the role of a great power. Those who envied the immunity from popular criticism that diplomats enjoyed in the chancelleries of Europe found it difficult to imagine that their own country could take an aggressive positive stand on anything amidst the discordant clamor of multitudes of diverse peoples. Imperceptibly they came to deny what had theretofore always been conceded in the United States — that public opinion ought properly to guide diplomacy. And, uncomfortable in that denial, they rested the blame on the divisions provoked by the foreigners.

Long before, Theodore Roosevelt had expressed his impatience with the cohesive ethnic groups that cluttered up his American scene. Now, eager for battle and loudest in the call for immediate participation, he denounced as un-American all who disagreed with his policies and criticized the Germans and Irish as hyphenates. (Although that designation never seemed to apply to the link in Anglo-American.) Stung by the old Rough-Rider's attacks, Wilson also turned upon dissenters from his policy. In 1915, he urged an audience of naturalized citizens in Philadelphia to become "thorough Americans" and warned them they could not do so if they thought of themselves in groups. "America does not consist of groups," he said. "A man who thinks of himself as belonging to a particular national group in America has not yet become an American." The relatively moderate terms in which the President spoke to a public audience concealed a deep underlying animus that could more clearly be perceived in the words of his ambassador to London. "We Americans," wrote Walter H. Page, "have got to . . . hang our Irish agitators and shoot our hyphenates and bring up our children with reverence for English history and in the awe of English literature." [5]

Such bitter sentiments gave the final impetus to the long-anticipated reversal of America's liberal immigration policy. The literacy test, often beaten before, and in 1915 again vetoed by President Wilson, finally passed over his objections in February 1917 amidst bitter denunciations of the Catholics, the Jews, the steamship companies, the capitalists, and the unskilled laborers. And this measure was no sooner passed than Representative Gardner of Massachusetts had introduced another to put absolute limits upon the number of new immigrants annually admissible under any circumstances. The restrictionists secured the enactment of the literacy test with the aid of adherents they had recruited through two decades of agitation, particularly with the aid of organized labor projected by prosperity and the manpower shortage to a position of unparalleled power and respectability. But most potent reinforcement of all was the fear of differences stirred up by almost three years of anxious argument over the war in Europe.

The same fears soon affected the very conduct of the war. Increasingly isolated by his duties from the sentiment of the mass of people, Wilson could not hold his followers to the idealistic line he had laid down. Humanitarian objectives were quickly pushed to the background in the press of the need for popularizing the conflict and for rousing the patriotic emotions of the citizenry. The Committee on Public Information, charged with the necessity of mobilizing public support, found itself steadily drawn to the use of propaganda not altogether compatible with the aims of the President.

To begin with, the committee stressed the 100 per cent Americanism of the war. This, it proclaimed, was an American undertaking, animated by purely American interests, one from which no patriot could dissent. The committee hoped thus to placate Middle Westerners still suspicious of Wilson's internationalism and to reassure Yankees and Southerners, impatient at his slowness in taking sides. The purpose of a good deal of its propaganda was to create and direct a completely united, a completely uniform, population. Capitalizing on the earlier attacks on hyphenated Americans, it pointed the finger of suspicion at any element in the society which seemed divided in loyalties; and it tended to interpret as a sign of divided loyalty any divergence from the ideal pattern to which it imagined the mass of Americans should conform.

The dilemma was that the conception of 100 per cent Americanism had to be flexible enough to justify association with the Allies and to quiet latent lingering antipathies to those countries. The overthrow of the Czar helped; the new Russia promised, for a time, to follow the liberal democratic path the United States had blazed. Romantic recollections of traditional friendship with France helped still more.

But it was a far more imposing task to counteract the inherited fear of England. Britain was the ancient enemy of 1776; every symbol and every act of American patriotism carried with it connotations hostile to Albion — the flag, the Star-Spangled Banner, the Declaration of Independence. Every recollection of the history book brought distrust of the king, the Union Jack, redcoats, perfidy during the Civil War. Even if the Irish had not added their own imported Anglophobia, it would have been an imposing task to convince Americans of the identity of their interests with those of England.

A good deal of energy went therefore to extolling English culture, and to tracing the indebtedness of the United States to it. The liberal democratic empire of George V, it was explained, was far removed from that of George III and close in aspirations to the transatlantic republic. The old argument of the unity of the Anglo-Saxons now became the touchstone of patriotism. Espousal of the Irish cause took on an anti-British and hence an un-American aspect. Indeed a federal judge expressed the belief, in banning a film entitled *The Spirit of 1776*, that any statement derogatory to Great Britain was a violation of the Espionage Act. The State Department, in the same vein, instructed the press that news unfavorable to England gave aid and comfort to the enemy.

As the draft, rising prices, and casualties brought home the seriousness of the war, popular attitudes began to change. It seemed easier to attain unity of effort through emphasis on the common hostility to the common foe than through repetition of the positive war aims. Partly through fear and partly through acceptance of the expedient, Wilson's original distinction between the German government and the German people dropped out of sight. Instead, "the words that won the war" violently attacked the whole nature of German culture, its music, its philosophy, even its food, as well as its political regime.

Led by the Committee on Public Information and urged on by the American Defense Society, the American Protective League, and similar patriotic organizations, the embattled citizens of the Republic drifted in an orgy of hatred. Attacks upon the German-American Alliance accused it of a nefarious plot to dominate the country through its "Kultur." Charges that it was a tool of the Kaiser ultimately forced the Alliance to dissolve. The Lutheran Church and its parochial schools and colleges were labeled undemocratic and un-American. Restrictions upon the press led to a sharp decline in the number of German newspapers published in the United States. Instruction in German all but disappeared from the schools where it had been planted as "a part of a plot formed by the German government to make the school children loyal to it." [6] Even where the language continued to be taught, public sentiment discouraged students and reduced enrollment. There were, in fact, communities where use of the hated tongue on the streets brought a fine. It was but a step to burning books and to banning Teutonic music; John Philip Sousa was pressed into service to compose a new wedding march that would replace the compositions of Wagner and Mendelssohn. Individuals and towns, and streets and public institutions found it safest to give their names some Anglo-Saxon form. All too often, the agitation culminated in violent riots against anyone suspected of a German taint. German-Americans could not help but feel the stings of the barbs directed against German culture.

The animus of such criticisms spread to every other group marked by foreignness. Once the Lutheran Church came under fire there was little inclination to differentiate among the nationalities of its adherents. Danes, Norwegians, and Swedes suffered along with the Germans. Any service in a language other than English soon was suspect, and in many places was actually forbidden.

All branches of the immigrant press came immediately under surveillance, partly because of the strange tongues in which most were published, partly because they were regarded in themselves as alien and untrustworthy. The German newspapers were not alone to be censored; the *Irish World*, the *Gaelic American*, and the *Irish Press* were, for a time, banned from the mails. Under the impact of war, many people felt the necessity of tightening the lines at home; and they were willing to accept any means toward that end. Responsible officials in the government deplored the extremes of popular action; but their only alternative was to create legal instruments to serve the same purpose. The stringent sedition laws thus aimed to mobilize a completely united population, made one by conformity.

Yet as a practical matter it was difficult to escape the presence of diverse elements in American society. It was true, for the time being, no group questioned the aims of the war, or indeed of the means by which those aims were furthered. The sedition laws made any deviation from established policy dangerous. Yet it was not enough simply to secure the passive acquiescence of these groups. The government desired their positive support, in recruiting men, in selling bonds, and in displaying the solidarity of the nation. For these reasons alone it was impelled to approach them on their own terms. But to communicate with them, it had to use the very foreign languages that elsewhere were being criticized as evidence of hyphenated loyalties.

The Committee on Public Information had early organized

a number of sections to work with foreign-language groups. These sections kept a watch over the opinions in newspapers and magazines and also disseminated the information that might strengthen the war effort. From twenty-three such divisions there flowed a steady stream of information. The argument reiterated again and again was that every group had a common stake in the struggle, and every group would profit from it. President Wilson had himself revealed the means. As the war proceeded, the doctrine of national self-determination acquired greater prominence and seemed to hold within it the promise of fulfilling many long-deferred hopes.

Self-determination, as the President had phrased it, bore a vaguely benevolent connotation; all men had the right to choose what government would rule them. For some Americans, the term would never be more clearly defined; it would continue to mean simply the extension to other parts of the world of their own kind of patriotism.

But for Americans with ethnic ties to Europe, the slogan had far greater impact. These groups of recent immigrants had only slowly been arriving at a conception of their own identity, laboriously worked out through the life of their societies and newspapers, through the pressure of rival churches and of intellectuals, through the bonds of familiar language. The attachment of these men to the place of their birth had little to do with political nationalism; and the occasional attempts to establish such a connection had little effect. Men joined the Polish National Alliance for the benefits it brought them in Pennsylvania, not from any conviction as to the future of central Europe. What had one matter to do with the other?

The call for self-determination defined and answered the whole problem. The sentiments that drew men together in lodges and that moved them to create their own churches had their source, they were told, in nationalism, the sense of loyalty that tied people to the state. The forms of that loyalty were abundantly clear from the patriotic Americanism of the United States. Every people ought to have an independent territorial homeland, an army, a flag, an anthem. Hastily, and as the symbol of their own participation in the war, Poles and Bohemians gave their support to invigorated nationalist movements. Paradoxically they were thus manifesting their own Americanism.

Wilson had probably not foreseen the consequences of the doctrine of self-determination. The United States had thus been slow to declare war on Austria; and when the break came in December 1917, the President had disavowed any intention of rearranging or impairing the integrity of the Hapsburg Empire.

He was not to carry out that resolution. French and British policy already called for dismemberment of the Dual Monarchy and the failure of negotiations for a separate peace gave additional weight to their views. Furthermore, the former subjects of the Empire by then envisioned independence as the product of the war. They had been vigorously enlisted in nationalist campaigns and their wishes could not easily be slighted in an election year.

The war thus clarified the relationships of Americans to the nascent Czechoslovak Republic. When the fighting had started in Europe in 1914, several immigrant groups had formed the Bohemian National Alliance, with headquarters in Chicago, to collect funds for the relief of war victims. The Alliance had established contact with the Czech leaders in Prague who were then campaigning for autonomy within the Austrian Empire.

For some time, the main issue remained unclear. The Bohemian Catholics in the United States were loyal to the Dual Monarchy. The Alliance, on the other hand, in 1916, was recruiting members for a Bohemian legion to fight in the Canadian Army, asking "for Bohemia the very thing which

America has always championed: rule of the people, for the people, and by the people." [7] Meanwhile ambitious Czech nationalists like Masaryk and Beneš, then in Paris, already had in view a state that would take in not Bohemia alone, but all the Czech lands (*pays tchèques*), and hoped to find the necessary support for that objective in the United States.

American entry into the war brought the issue into focus. The summons to take a part in the struggle found the Bohemian-Americans responsive. And what better means was there of striking at the common enemy Austria than to assist the Czech nationalists? Voyta Beneš mobilized the opinion of the group; Father Zlamal persuaded the Catholics to join the movement; and an agreement with the Slovaks in Pittsburgh in effect delineated the future outlines of the new republic. What had once been a vague aspiration now acquired the concreteness and drive of a crusade that swept along the American government. Congressman Sabath of Chicago who sought Wilson's support had at first found the President apathetic. By the summer of 1918, however, the movement had grown in strength and Tumulty, Wilson's secretary, had taken the initiative in bringing the President to support it. There remained to be settled only the details of the peace. But that was an end worth fighting for.

For other groups too, self-determination gave a meaning to the war that brushed away lingering uncertainties as to their own identities and that enabled them, as patriotic Americans, to enlist in a variety of campaigns of national liberation. Heartened by a mild declaration from Secretary of State Lansing, in June 1918, Croats and Slovenes in the United States became partisans of the new Yugoslavia; and there was talk of drawing a Yugoslav division from among the doughboys in General Pershing's command. The perplexing Polish question now fell into place. Until the war, the Pulaski Legion of America had attracted only a few members with its talk of Poland reborn. Even after Sarajevo when a gleam of hope appeared, there were divisions of opinion as to whether the new state should arise under Allied or Austrian auspices. But the Fourteen Points settled all doubts. The reference to Poland was vague, *Ameryka-Echo* (Toledo) explained, but it pointed the direction in which Polish-Americans were to labor. Meanwhile the former subjects of Russia's Baltic provinces were finding roles in other movements that would create new republics. Shortly, Alexander Bilmanis would leave Nebraska and go on to become president of Lithuania, while the hopes of other Americans would fasten on events in Latvia and Estonia.

The formula of democratic self-determination allowed even enemy aliens to purge themselves of the guilt of their emperors. The process was relatively simple for some groups. The men who had until 1917 agitated for a strong Albania under Turkey now campaigned for the support of the Allies. The Hungarians, formerly loyal to the Hapsburgs, now turned against the old order; with the aid of the Committee on Public Information, Alexander Konta formed the American Hungarian Loyalty League in the expectation that victory for the United States would bring freedom for the Magyars.

The most striking effects were upon the Germans. Under the impact of the declaration of war and of the violent propaganda against Kaiser and Kultur, all seemed at first lost. The press and the German-American Alliance hastened to make protestations of their loyalty; but dismay, fear, resentment at the rebuff by other Americans combined in the conviction it was no longer possible to maintain the identity of the group. The Joplin *Turnverein*, disbanding, conceded, "Our countrymen cannot and will not and should not be expected to countenance the existence of our Verein." [8]

But the Committee on Public Information itself helped restore the confidence of the German-Americans whose support it needed at home and for the sake of the propaganda directed at Germany. With its aid in 1917, the Friends of

German Democracy took up the work of converting the German-Americans to the Allied cause. Through meetings and publications it argued that the interests of the Fatherland would best be served by an Allied victory. Although continued public hostility kept the group from ever acquiring a large membership, the Friends of German Democracy demonstrated that the conception of democratic self-determination could make German nationalism compatible with American patriotism.

The Irish-Americans, old partners in the struggle for neutrality, also found self-determination the key to adjustment to the new situation. Their Anglophobia had become dangerous; it exposed them to criticism as slackers and made them seem responsible for the continued agitation in Ireland that hampered the war effort. But given the principle of self-determination, a free Ireland might actually be an outcome of the war. Wilson himself realized that principles apply differently to friends and enemies and was irked with the impatience of the Irish. He hoped the British, in the general settlement at the end of the war, would voluntarily make some concession. The Irish-Americans wanted immediate proof of England's good intentions. But in any case, they were certain that, whether England willed it or not, the war was Ireland's opportunity to exercise the right to self-determination and independence.

The desperate hope to which men clutched was that some ultimate good might come forth from the known evils of war. In the troublesome times that brought the disasters of the Old World even to the homes of the New, it was tempting to believe that the peace would restore the values of fraternity and unity by bringing to fulfillment the national aspirations of all peoples. In the United States all men longed for faith in that fulfillment — the Italians and Greeks for the redemption of lost territories, the Ukrainians and Armenians for the recovery of ancient sovereignties.

All peoples — even those, like the Jews and Negroes, for whom the very conception of political nationalism had been strange. Few Jews before 1914 had given thought to the vague notion they might ever constitute a state. Those long settled in the United States had accepted the dictum of Isaac M. Wise that "America is our Zion"; and the recently-arrived had made their choice in the process of migration; this was their promised land.[9] The charitably-minded contributed to the support of institutions in the Holy Land. But only a handful of sentimentalists subscribed to the Zionist doctrines then being agitated in Europe.

The war made a difference. Immediately it created a tremendous problem of relief in eastern Europe and in Palestine, where an embryonic community was cut off from the remittances that had supported it. Sensitive to the needs of their oppressed coreligionists, often of their own families still in Europe, American Jews mustered their resources for immediate aid; until 1917 as citizens of the only great neutral power, they were most capable of bearing the burden. American entry into the war posed the necessity of taking a position on the peace settlement that would affect the future of millions of European Jews. And the Balfour Declaration of November 1917, for the first time, gave substance to the shadowy dreams of a national Jewish homeland.

These pressures which made Americans the leaders of world Jewry awakened many to a sense of the obligations of their affiliation; such men as Louis D. Brandeis now felt the necessity of taking a more active role in these matters. The same pressures also created uneasiness as to the loose organization of the Jewish community. As among other ethnic groups there arose the demand for a central guiding body that would draw together the scattered, divided organizations and provide them with an effective voice in influencing national policy.

The multitude of philanthropic, religious, and fraternal

associations until then had mirrored the diversity of America's Jews. The American Jewish Committee, formed in 1906 to defend the rights of Jews throughout the world, was a self-constituted group that represented only a minority of long-established Jews. It could not speak for the more recent immigrants or for the Zionists. In 1914, the Committee, with a number of other organizations, had sponsored the Joint Distribution Committee for the limited purpose of administering relief funds. But as time went on, the argument was more frequently advanced that Jews needed a representative body to speak for their national interests. An attempt to convoke such a Congress in 1916 failed. Yet sentiment in favor of the step mounted. Only thus, it was argued, could the rights of Jews be safeguarded in the approaching peace settlement.

To the Negroes of America the war brought home the implications of a massive change in situation. In April 1917, the great northward migration was already well under way. Thousands of Southern colored men had seen their new Canaans in Chicago, New York, and Philadelphia; yet they had learned that the move alone would not solve all their problems. With Northern freedom came also the life of the urban slums, the responsibility of earning a livelihood, and the difficult adjustment to inequalities subtler than those of the familiar Jim Crow.

In the dislocations in which all Americans were involved, the Negroes still found themselves singled out for the most violent attack. In the year the war came, ugly riots flared in East St. Louis and in Chester, Pennsylvania. In August 1917, colored soldiers engaged in a pitched battle with the police of Houston; and the conviction by court martial and speedy execution of thirteen black men revived memories of the Brownsville affray, revived the uneasiness that even the uniform of the United States Army did not clothe the Negro with the rights and dignities of men. When the draft policy shunted them into segregated divisions, almost invariably under white officers, denied commissions to colored doctors, and refused the services of colored nurses, that uneasiness became a source of tormenting anxieties. What had the war to do with them?

Expected to serve in spite of the injustices accorded them, the Negroes were more and more often to ask what it was that set them off as a group. The answer was not as simple in the North as in the South where the blacks were merely the submerged sector of a whole society, held off from the dominant remainder by a compulsory pattern of segregation and obedience. For those who moved in these years, the very act of departure revealed they did have some power of choice; their place was not unalterably fixed. Above the Mason-Dixon line, they discovered, and took part in, churches and societies that held together out of the will of the members. The newcomers encountered men of their own color, born in the North or migrants from the West Indies, who had never lived under the Southern restrictions and were not content to accept inferiority of status. Here were some men with capital who invested in real estate and conducted businesses and had ambitions and realized them, and who clearly were not simply the lowest sector of society.

The fact that society counted all blacks alike did not to the Negroes account for their identity as a group. Not only were they aware of meaningful divisions among themselves, but admission that pressure from without drove them together was an acknowledgment of their dependence upon the will of outsiders. For people anxious to establish the sense of their independence, it was more satisfying to think they held together because they found positive values in affiliation within the group.

The descendants of the old Boston or Philadelphia Negro families by no means felt themselves one with the laborers fresh from the fields of Alabama or, for that matter, with the aggressive Jamaican. Even among the recent arrivals, little

associations were likely to set themselves off — the Sons of
Georgia or the Carolina Societies. But there was also an overriding sense of identity that drew them all together; and a
variety of explanations accounted for it.

Some Negroes, impressed by the diversity characteristic of
all American society, had come to think of themselves as
one of the many groups distinguished by common immigrant
antecedents. They compared themselves with Jewish-Ameri-
cans, or German-Americans, or Italian-Americans. They were
in that sense Afro-Americans.

Others accepted the meaning whites gave their color, but
with a different evaluation. Their blackness was a sign of
heredity that marked them off as a race, only not as a stigma,
but as a distinction. They were, a Negro Catechism declared,
"of all races the most favored by the Muses of Music, Poetry
and Art . . . possessed of those qualities of courage, honor,
and intelligence necessary to . . . the most brilliant development of the human species." Their "Race Patriotism," justified
by "noble origins, splendid achievements and ancient cultures"
would redress the temporary abasement from which they
suffered.[10]

The Negroes who now nurtured pride of color were
already conscious of kinship with other men similarly marked
throughout the world. The war heightened that consciousness. The Harlem doughboys fell in with dark-skinned
French colonials. Learning of the difficulties of imperialism,
they were inclined to hope they might find allies "among
those whom the white man also oppresses because of their
black or yellow skins." Faced with common problems, was
it not proper to expect that all colored peoples should "learn
to think together as one race, one family"? [11]

In the immediate hour of the nation's peril, they would
demonstrate their loyalty by postponing a reckoning of their
grievances. They would serve "the flag that set us free" and
acquiesce, for the time being, in the discrimination directed

against them.[12] But they had the right to expect that peace would bring its reward. Was there not for them also, as for the Pole and the Czech, the Irishman and the Jew, a promise in the national self-determination that the President had said would be the outcome of the war?

They were not then different from those other Americans who sought the same meaning in the war. The monumental costs of this great struggle could not be without some purpose. Their government told them what they wished to hear, that the purpose was to restore that for which their hearts most longed, fraternity and unity. But it was in the nature of the war and of the hatreds it fanned that a prideful nationalism should be taken as the form of fraternity and as the source of unity.

For the time being, participation in the common effort absorbed every energy. There might be hints now and then that if the Italian-Americans were to be satisfied along the Adriatic, the Croat-Americans might not be, that Greek-American and Albanian-American claims might be incompatible, that there might not be enough rewards to satisfy all the eager claimants. But confidence in the peace that all so anxiously attended quieted every doubt; the troubled men who fought and worked fixed their eyes upon the approaching day when the end would come to strife and oppression and the world would be safe for democracy through self-determination.

CHAPTER VI

Postwar Era

The war ended. The fighting men laid down their arms and all the energies mobilized for the struggle slackened. It was a time for reaping the fruits of victory.

Only, there were no fruits. Peace did not come. In the aftermath, all the tensions and sacrifices of war brought forth no more than a pervasive sense of betrayal. Those dubious from the start found their inner doubts justified; those who had been imbued with Wilson's ideals found their faith shattered.

Realization of the bitter outcome came slowly through the months of discussion that followed the armistice. When Wilson went first to Paris he carried still with him the hopes of an enduring settlement that would earn Americans the gratitude of a world they had saved for democracy. The Hun had been decisively beaten, his military power absolutely crushed. There seemed no reason why the war's objectives could not at once be attained.

To most Americans, who followed at a distance the progress of the negotiations, the main objective was to prevent the rebirth of the German tyranny that had been the cause of so much misery. There was concern lest the Prussians mask their intentions of continuing the struggle for world mastery by a superficial adherence to the ideals of human brotherhood; there were fears lest the Fourteen Points permit the Germans to escape too easily and to regain by other means what they had lost in battle. The people who had so often been told of the menace of the Kaiser's Kultur were not willing to believe that the change of regime was more than an expedient to soften the impact of defeat. They were not willing, as the Venango *Herald* put it, to "go without one more helping of meat to feed the brutes who ravaged Belgium, the savages who bayoneted little children. . . ." [1] Before long there would be complaints the war had ended too soon — without the devastation of German cities. Now, however, all the aims of the fighting seemed realizable with defeat of the common enemy.

The sense that all rewards were within grasp animated particularly the nationalist societies of every sort that had flourished through the war. From every part of Europe, the leaders of would-be states had descended upon the Peace Conference, urging their recently defined historic claims for self-determination. Conscious of the weight Americans would bring to bear upon the resolution of these grave issues, all drew upon whatever support they could muster. In the hotels of Paris, a *Times* reporter encountered a Yugoslav diplomat who had been a newspaperman in the United States, a Lithuanian who had been a lawyer in Detroit, a Syrian from Washington Street, and a Czech who had once peddled sculptured figures in the streets of America. Back across the Atlantic thousands of eager supporters waited impatiently for news of their new dreams come true.

All were disappointed, adherents of the victors as well as adherents of the vanquished. It was not in dreams the pattern of the settlement took form, but in the cold calculations of statesmen eyeing the national advantage.

Whatever hopes the Germans may have had that the Kaiser's guilt would not extend to the new republic, they were quickly disillusioned.

At Versailles, they were called upon to bear the whole onus of the war. The responsibility for that guilt spread across the

ocean, touched all those who shared their heritage. It effaced
the efforts of the Friends of German Democracy to restore
faith in their culture. The animus against the German-Americans persisted to discredit their language, religion, press, and
institutions.

It was well enough to demonstrate the continuing loyalty of
the group, to be more American than other Americans,
through the Carl Schurz Foundation and the Steuben Society
to establish a connection with the American past. But it was
difficult to still a profound, if infrequently expressed, resentment against their mistreatment. In the election of 1920, the
German-American vote turned heavily against the Democratic Party and against the League of Nations as a sign of that
resentment. And in the decade that followed the organizations,
shattered by the war, were slow to recover, partly because
they were no longer adequate to the needs of their old members, partly because the old members were reluctant to dis-
play those needs openly.

The peace meant a rebuff also for people whose national
aspirations were completely frustrated. A most favorable public sentiment had lulled Armenian- and Ukrainian-Americans
into security. For a time indeed legations in Washington had
been visible evidence of the existence of those two governments. But neither state materialized, to the consternation of
their supporters in the United States. The Armenians splin-
tered into factions, divided amongst themselves by political
differences. The Ukrainians lapsed into a profound confusion
as to their own identity; while some continued to think of
themselves as Ukrainians, others began to wonder whether
they were not, after all, kinds of Russians, or perhaps, Galicians.

Nor was there satisfaction in partial fulfillment. As the war
ended, Irish-Americans looked to the Peace Conference for
independence. Distrusting Wilson, they nevertheless hoped
that their political strength and the logic of his own ideas

would compel him to act on their behalf. The President had indeed long wished that the British would appease their intransigent Irish subjects, although diplomatically he made no public statement to that effect.

At Paris, however, this question receded in importance; it was remote from the major preoccupations of the Conference. Easily enough, Wilson accepted the English contention that the Irish problem was purely a domestic one. On his first return to the United States he was with great reluctance induced to see a delegation from the Irish Race Convention; and, at that, insulted Judge Cohalan and gave the Irish no hope whatsoever. They could hardly have been surprised that the ultimate settlement contained not a word about Ireland.

That was not the worst of it. The Covenant of the League of Nations contained within it a threat that might stand permanently in the way of Irish independence. Under Article X of the Covenant, the United States, were it a member, could never, in the event of an uprising, aid those fighters for freedom in Ireland; indeed it might conceivably be called upon to assist the oppressors who were even then crushing a revolution in the Emerald Isle. Dismayed and angered, the Irish-Americans bitterly fought ratification of the "English scheme for a League of Nations." [2]

Within Ireland itself there was no waiting. Depending upon themselves alone, *Sinn Fein*, the republicans had organized a provisional government under Eamon de Valera and were busily fighting out the issue with the Black and Tan British constabulary. As terror enveloped the island, Irish-Americans increased their agitation through both the moderate American Association for the Recognition of the Irish Republic and the radical Friends of Irish Freedom. At the end of 1921 came the compromise that created the Irish Free State, a nation not altogether independent and not altogether whole. Whatever its effect at home, the adjustment only confused Irish-Americans. The Friends of Irish Freedom indignantly rejected this final ruse of perfidious Albion. Although de Valera acquiesced, he remained outside the government, refusing to take the oath of allegiance; and as long as he did so, his American followers remained unhappy over partition and over the surviving ties to the British Empire.

For many groups, there remained an unredeemed province for which no other gain could compensate. Vilna, grabbed off by the Poles, lingered in the complaints of the Lithuanian-Americans; and frustration of Italian ambitions along the Adriatic drove the Federation of Italian Societies of America to order its members to "sustain the Republican ticket as a protest against President Wilson . . . for the shameful mistreatment" of Italy.[3]

For the Jews, the great hopes touched off by Wilson's promises were almost totally frustrated. As the war drew to a close, the Jews of the United States felt the immediate pressure of many needs. In the desolated regions of eastern Europe, their persecuted coreligionists struggled for mere physical survival; in the new nations they lacked elemental political and civic rights; and the dream of the Zionists for a national home in Palestine, now apparently on the point of realization, called for some concrete support.

The Joint Distribution Committee, organized during the war, carried out the monumental task of rescuing the remnants of east European Jewry from starvation. In the six years after 1914, it disbursed almost $40,000,000 in relief.

But charity alone could not rehabilitate these stricken communities. In the interregnum that followed the collapse of the German, Austrian, and Russian empires, the Jews had been profoundly dislocated; a series of pogroms in Poland and Hungary deprived some of their lives and a wave of economic boycotts deprived many more of their livelihoods. A Congress of American Jewish organizations, including the American Jewish Committee, had convened in December 1918, and had sent a delegation to the Peace Conference to coöperate with the Jews of other countries in securing international recognition of the right of Jews to equality throughout the world. The result of their efforts was the incorporation in the treaties that organized the new states of eastern Europe of provisions guaranteeing the civil and religious rights of Jews and other minorities. Alas, the delegates had hardly returned to the United States in 1920 when reactions throughout the Continent made it clear these provisions would be honored in the breach rather than in the observance.

Nor was the hope of a national home in Palestine to relieve these disappointments. The Balfour Declaration had at first been welcomed by Zionists and non-Zionists alike. In its loose terminology, the former could find the promise of an ultimate state and the latter no more than encouragement of a center for the pursuit and development of literature, science, and art in a Jewish environment. It was soon apparent there were substantial differences between these conceptions. In 1922, the Zionists, growing in strength and impatient with the reserved attitude of the American Jewish Committee, moved to act independently in the United States and created a new American Jewish Congress. By then, however, they had found it no easier to get on with European Zionists than with American non-Zionists; a transatlantic struggle for control had resulted in the victory of the Europeans. Certainly unfolding events made it difficult to hold to the faith that mere satisfaction of territorial ambitions in Palestine would bring a solution of the Jewish problem.

The experience of other groups demonstrated that even satisfaction of every territorial ambition had its drawbacks. The Czechs and Poles had been thus gratified, but now found themselves embroiled, at home and in the United States, with minorities of Germans, Slovaks, Ruthenians, Russians, Ukrainians, and Jews. The Greeks held an uneasy hold on Smyrna and yet were learning from America that the Bulgarians and Macedonians who had emigrated from Thrace, and Albanians from northern Epirus were begging their brethren to rebel at Greek annexation.

Nothing came up to expectations. Hopefully little groups of exiles went back from the United States to live under the new regimes in Hungary, Finland, Romania, and Czechoslovakia. But their own governments proved disquietingly unstable, unwilling to effect the reforms Americans anticipated, and subject to violent disturbances. It was not long before many of these men were making still a third Atlantic crossing.

Even, it proved, those like the Albanian-Americans who had substantial power in the new government! The Albanian-Americans had been pro-Turk and pro-German before 1917. But the fortunes of Allied politics dictated there was to be a free Albania. Back to run the new state went several thousand residents of Massachusetts, only to find in a succession of disillusioning experiences that self-determination solved more problems in anticipation than in practice.

Many Americans with close ties to Europe could ascribe their dissatisfaction to specific national issues. But the disappointment that spread over the United States, as the exuberance of the Armistice subsided, was more general. A vague but poignant sense of discouragement that the sacrifices of the war had not been justified by its results spread over the country.

Negroes everywhere, but especially in the bulging cities to which so many had recently migrated, were determined that the war was an end and, also, a beginning. A series of race riots in Chicago, Washington, D. C., Omaha, East St. Louis, and Springfield, Ohio, in 1919 and 1920 quickly let the black men know that if, indeed, a new world was coming, they would have to shape it themselves. Many turned to a Back to Africa movement, proclaiming Marcus Garvey "provisional president" of the Black Republic, and leader of all the black people of the world. Others, who remained skeptical of Garvey's scheme, nevertheless condoned it as a symbol of the new militancy of the Negro.

In the Middle West, where many men had only reluctantly
been converted to the necessity of entering the struggle, the
hope of some great moral outcome had quieted the pacifist
doubts to which Bryan had given expression. There the peace
was a defeat and a betrayal; power politics had clearly outweighed the idealistic ends of international democracy for
which they had fought. Did that not call into question the
validity of the ends themselves? Substantial elements in this
region turned against the League, and remorselessly helped to
strike it down.

But even in the East where Yankees and Southerners had
welcomed American entry into the war on behalf of Anglo-
Saxon unity there was a growing suspicion that Wilson had
bungled the great opportunity. With the rejection of the
Treaty, uneasiness mounted to certainty. The United States
had failed to take advantage of the occasion; the struggle had
been in vain.

The unhappiness with which all men, everywhere, accepted
the peace was a sign that the war had failed to resolve the
problems over which it had been fought. It was also a sign of
the awareness that the war had not at all lessened the gravity
of the older difficulties and tensions under which the country
had earlier labored — if anything those had grown weightier.

To Americans who recalled the agitation of the Populists,
there was a familiar quality to the rekindled agrarian grievances. Until 1919, farm prices had risen steadily, during the
war, astronomically. Now came a total collapse. Having invested heavily in equipment (the number of tractors grew
from 1,000 in 1910 to 246,000 in 1920), the farmer was subject
to heavy fixed charges and incapable of adjusting to the
diminution of his income. Mortgages, foreclosure, tenancy
mounted rapidly.

Nor was industry better prepared to maintain the high point
of output it reached during the war. Foreign competition and
the contraction of domestic markets lowered the levels of pro-

duction, brought back unemployment. A depression to match that of 1907 seemed in the making.

Labor was unsettled socially as well as economically. During the war New York, Chicago, Detroit, Los Angeles, and other cities had grown phenomenally; the drift of population from rural regions had compensated in part for the halt to immigration. The supply of housing, however, had not kept pace with this growth and the decline of earnings while prices remained high evoked complaints of the oppressive cost of living and complicated the old problems of disease, vice, and crime. In the working-class districts of the cities, inhabited by strangers and strange in their very aspect to other Americans, there stirred a profound unrest as resentful men took stock of their situation. And outside those districts there gathered a vast uneasiness at what those hemmed-in men might do.

With organized labor determined not to retreat from the position it had attained during the war, and with the great industrialists determined to settle once and for all the question of mastery, an irrepressible conflict between capital and labor rose ominously above the horizon in 1919. The decisive day came when 300,000 steelworkers, with the support of the American Federation of Labor, walked out on strike. The steel strike proved that the most helpless among American laborers insisted upon relief from their helplessness, even if that involved a direct assault upon the citadel of conservative American capitalism.

The strike was important as much for its failure as for what it attempted to achieve. The steel corporations fought it relentlessly, fearful that the slightest concession would undermine their whole position. The intransigent opposition of the corporations defeated the union and dealt labor a blow from which it did not recover for fourteen years. The dwindling membership roles of the organized labor movement reflected how penetrating that blow had been.

There was also a particular significance to the means used

to crush the strike. The mill owners stopped at nothing. Their importation of Negro scab labor from the South injected the racial issue into the conflict, and poisoned the relationships between whites and blacks in this industry for a long time to come. But the most destructive weapon was the accusation that the strike was "not based upon specific grievances, but is aimed at the overthrow of American institutions and ideals just as surely as if a Bolshevist army was marching on Washington."[4] Other industrialists quickly joined the steel tycoons in giving currency to the false charges that the radicals had maliciously precipitated the strike. They thus helped to generate the great red scare that swept across the nation in the next five years.

The fear of radicals was then not unfamiliar. Back in the first years of the century the anarchists had already acquired their unenviable reputation. The assassination of McKinley in 1901 had fixed in peoples' minds the picture of the bomb-throwing anarchist. And the activities of the I.W.W. before 1917 had strengthened that picture. The I.W.W. had vigorously resisted the war, and had been the only substantial element openly and consistently disloyal to the government. Some socialists had also opposed the war, including E. V. Debs, their presidential candidate, who went to jail for his opinions. In the popular view, this fact identified all Socialists with the Wobblies.

The red scare had reached new heights in 1917 as the Bolsheviks took power in Russia. It was not the Revolution as such that antagonized America; indeed, the removal of the Czar had first been welcomed as a sign the war was already achieving its democratizing ends. Rather it was the Bolshevik determination to make a separate peace with Germany that turned Americans against them. This determination established two connections in the minds of Americans. In the first place it made the Bolsheviks equivalent to the I.W.W. and to the other dissident elements in America, all traitors to American ideals, all alike. In the second place it popularized the charge that the whole revolution had been an elaborate German plot and that the Bolsheviks, in some mysterious way, were acting as tools of the German government.

Through the closing stages of the war to the early years of the peace while American soldiers were actually stationed at Archangel and in Siberia, the hatred of the new regime and of anyone associated with it mounted. Elihu Root, back from a fruitless mission to Russia in August 1917, had announced that there were men in America "who ought to be taken out at sunrise and shot for treason." [5] The lurid stories of atrocities intensified the feeling that everything had gotten out of hand abroad, and that the enemy was already within the gates at home.

The personal ambitions of Attorney General A. Mitchell Palmer may have given the red scare its early form. But the intensity and continued vigor of the movement to root the radicals out of American life sprang from widespread popular fears that could be satisfied with nothing less than total loyalty; and loyalty, now that the war was over, meant conformity — 100 per cent Americanism. Government investigations set themselves the task of eliminating every disloyal, pro-German, Bolshevik element in American life. Outside the government, self-constituted groups of patriots determined to do extralegally what the law could not do. The veterans organized in the American Legion felt the call of this mission with particular earnestness and recognized few limits on their right or duty to fight the Reds. Before long, Wilson's *New Freedom* was banned in Nebraska in the name of the Americanism he had fought to preserve.

The fear was of a dream's end. Out of the past the parading men had brought hope of a society in which human dignity would extend to its every dimension. This was their meaning of democracy; for this they had wished to make the world safe.

Their present set against them forbidding odds. In hazarding their dream against the world, they had been defeated. But they had thereby been weakened also at home. Everywhere about them, the canons of accepted decency seemed to topple. It was as if the failure to achieve the ideal in its totality had brought the ideal itself into question. To the youngsters of Scott Fitzgerald's generation what could not be done well need not be done at all. Prohibition emphasized the evils of intemperance; family life rocked with the rise in the divorce rate and the new liberty in sexual matters; and the great cities seemed open to the unrestrained depradation of gangsters and to the turbulence of mob violence. How frail the barrier between civilization and the primal jungle!

And how marked the contrast with the past! In the shiny pictures of the *Saturday Evening Post* were still the orderly little towns, with every man in his proper place, and villainy and virtue clearly distinguished. An overwhelming nostalgia took hold of those weary of change. Let only the few wrong turnings be retraced and the safety of the past might be redeemed.

A stubborn insistence that the change had not been decisive animated these years. At Dayton, Bryan heatedly defied the science that made less of man by connecting him to the monkey. In the upsurge of piety for the past, it seemed only necessary to reaffirm the old virtues through law and order, and through a determined clinging to the ancient verities.

The enemies took clear form. Not from within had the old life cracked, but from the insidious outsiders, at home and abroad. Maintenance of law and order required, first of all, vigilance against these foes. American xenophobia had many sources. In some families there lingered recollections of earlier outbreaks — of the A.P.A. or the Know-Nothings. The conviction that the war had been a betrayal and the League, a failure, added animosity against the foreigners responsible for both. Distrust mounted against every tie that might lead America into the pitfalls of the world beyond its borders. The

World Court went the way of the League, suspect as an en-
tangling alliance.

Most often, however, the general search for an enemy without to unite the group within focused upon the foreign-born.
Although the aliens had been completely loyal through the
war, "the meanness of chauvinism," the "brutalities of prejudice," and "the short sightedness of ignorance" had convicted
them of unfaithfulness. "Not a pin dropt in the home of anyone with a foreign name but that it rang like thunder on the
inner ear of some listening sleuth," George Creel recalled.[6]
Vigilant citizens cried out against their incompletely Americanized neighbors, against the very existence of foreign languages, the foreign press, and the foreign pulpit.

The drive to Americanize the immigrant continued after the
war. In 1919, the laws of fifteen states prohibited instruction
in foreign languages. There were efforts to close the mails to
publications not in English. Within the Department of Justice, the Citizens' Protective Association, an organization of
volunteer spies, did much to destroy the confidence of the
foreign born.

The Red Scare fed distrust of the immigrant; by now the
alien had become identified with the radical. Earlier in the
century, the strange names of a few anarchists had not obscured the essentially indigenous quality of American radical
movements. Just before the war, the outbreaks of labor violence in Paterson and Lawrence had roused a flutter of in-
dignation against the Italians and French-Canadians, unappre-
ciative of their places. Russian Communism contributed to the
uneasiness. But the conviction that it was foreigners who men-
aced the American Way rested not so much on any rational
examination of evidence, as on the will to regard as one the
two seeming threats to the old order of society. Thus it became clear, as its Master informed the National Grange in
1919, that the nation's troubles were due to "the fact that too
many people are in America who are not of America."[7]

The Palmer raids had singled out the foreign-born as particularly vulnerable victims, had denied them access to the courts and to the ordinary processes of law. Ugly deportations and arbitrary arrests not only injured the individuals affected but also created the panicky mood in which Congress passed the Sterling-Johnson Act of 1920 to rid the country of aliens who advocated overthrow of the government. Immigrants now lived in the United States on sufferance, Herbert Hoover told the Poles of Buffalo, and would be tolerated only if they behaved.

The Sacco-Vanzetti Case was climactic. Hatred of the radicals and the foreign-born sent these Italians to the execution chamber; and the long agitation of the case perpetuated the notion that all Italians were anarchists.

All that was foreign was suspect. But it was no simple matter to see through the various guises of un-Americanism. The alert patriot fought on many fronts. Even proof of citizenship or of nativity was no safe guide.

The earlier image of the Jew as the mysterious immigrant stranger, related to the world of finance, now took on a more sinister appearance. Connected, as before the war, with the city through commerce which was its lifeblood, the Jew attracted much of the fear and suspicion the city aroused. Now, one of Fitzgerald's heroes

> read a dozen Jewish names on a line of stores; in the door of each stood a dark little man watching the passers from intent eyes — eyes gleaming with suspicion, with pride, with clarity, with cupidity, with comprehension . . . The slow upward creep of this people—the little stores, growing, expanding . . . was impressive — in perspective it was tremendous.[8]

To stem the slow upward creep, other Americans resorted to a subtle pattern of discrimination — in employment and in access to the opportunities for professional training. President

Lowell's open demand for a quota on Jewish students at Harvard was never adopted; but it was clear that many colleges achieved the same end through less formal means.

The enemy was dangerous and strong and operated on two fronts. Through control of finance and the power of gold, his bankers manipulated the world's wealth. Through the Bolsheviks the Jew schemed to draw from among the laborers the mass army with which he would overthrow existing governments; the Russian Revolution had already shown what a group of "East Side Jews" could do.

A little book that reached the United States just after the war revealed the inner nature of this threatening group. The *Protocols of the Elders of Zion* unmasked an insidious conspiracy of Jews to subvert Christian civilization and to assume control of the world. This was the master key that explained the many mysteries of recent history, the disastrous wars and revolutions, the failures of peace, the corruption of morals, and the collapse of traditional standards.

No matter if the book was early proved a forgery and if no shred of evidence substantiated its wild statements. To people eager for some logical explanation for the bewildering events that had swept them along for a decade, it offered a satisfying scheme with a wild rationality of its own. It thus convinced Henry Ford, whose shrewd practicality had coped with all the problems of creating a great industry but who was utterly at a loss to understand his own times. Recalling the long series of encounters with Wall Street bankers, brooding over the incomprehensible collapse of his peace mission, and troubled by disruptive labor difficulties, Ford embraced the suggestion that a single cause accounted for all. Responsible for the numerous pinpricks and the painful wounds of his — of America's — life was the one menace, the International Jew. Destroy this enemy and a return to the old, healthy ways would be possible.

Except that sometimes the enemy took another form. The crowds of foreigners who streamed up the steps of the Catholic

Church, the priests and nuns in alien garb, were they not all in their cathedrals and convents in communion with a foreign power? For Protestant Americans there was a sense of mystery and discomfort about the half-known rites of the Church; there was a vagueness as to the nature of the attachment of American Catholics to the Vatican; there was, increasingly, suspicion of the international ties that held the hierarchy and the strange orders together.

During the war, there had been occasional attacks upon the Pope as a tool of the Austrian Empire, as an agent of European despotism. After the war, there was a tendency to transfer the animus against the Irish and Italians to their church. But the critical question was whether other Americans could depend upon the loyalty of those with international religious affiliations.

In 1924 the issue came squarely before the country with the possibility that a Catholic son of Irish immigrants might be candidate for president. Through the heated sessions of the Democratic National Convention, through more than one hundred indecisive ballotings, the whispered question spread outward through the watching nation, raising everywhere uneasy doubts.

Four years later the issue was more openly joined. Alfred E. Smith was then Democratic candidate; and for his defeat were mobilized all the anti-Catholic sentiments. Despite his declaration that there was no incompatibility between Catholic religious doctrines and American political democracy, he was attacked as the instrument of a plot that would deliver the country to the control of the Pope and make the United States "the tail of the Roman Catholic kite." The violent propaganda of the campaign created an image of Catholicism as a menace because of its strangeness, its alliance with corrupt machine politics, its encouragement of intemperance and hostility to prohibition, and its internationalism.

Anti-Semitism and anti-Catholicism defined the true American; only the native Protestant could be relied upon to stand firm against every external threat. The Jews and the Catholics were not feared and fought simply because so many of them had been born outside the United States. It was not even because both had international connections. They seemed dangerous because they were foreign in that they failed to conform to the inner image other Americans carried with them of what the American ought to be. Perhaps the Massachusetts Yankee, the Georgia Cracker, and the Indiana Hoosier would not have recognized one another's image. But for that very reason they strove to establish the sense of their identity by contrasting themselves with the nonconforming outsiders. Only thus could they merge back into a reassuring group, whole and capable of bringing relief from the perplexities of their lives.

The longing for conformity, already stimulated by the war and by the effort to Americanize the immigrants, was now transformed by the racist assumptions that influenced American thinking.

The conception that mankind was not one, but divided into distinct races, separated from each other by the biological characteristics of their blood, had already received some currency before 1916. The color line had acquainted many Americans with the notion; imperialist expansion in the Far East and in the Caribbean brought it home to others. Furthermore this had been a common subject of discussion among sociologists, anthropologists, and geneticists who had given racism a widespread academic respectability.

But in 1916 the whole idea came dramatically to public notice through a book published with the most respectable scholarly credentials. In *The Passing of the Great Race*, Madison Grant of the American Museum of Natural History explained how the original Aryan stock responsible for European civilization had been corrupted by inferior peoples. The United States which had reached the apogee of its culture in 1860 had been deteriorating ever since with the infusion into its blood streams of alien strains. In the years after the war the same theme was expounded by such eugenicists as Lothrop Stoddard and by such historians as Burton Hendrick and H. J. Eckenrode.

In the ever widening circle of readers for these lurid books were troubled people who sought in the oneness of blood the oneness they lacked in the lives of their communities. The stability and security they could not attain from family and neighborhood they hoped to attain in the wider blood-group, the race. Unhappily, race in a folk of such heterogeneous antecedents could not be defined by any tracing of ancestry but only by the exclusion of those denominated outsiders — the Negro, the Jew, the Catholic. Behind the dread of intermarriage and the mixtures of bloods, behind the accusations against the sensuous black, the lecherous Semite, and the "unmarried bucks of the Pope" lurked the nameless dreads of men who were alone, cut off from their past, cut off from one another.[9]

It was such men also who sought refuge in the hooded conclaves of the Klan. That organization, founded in 1915 with the name of its Reconstructionist predecessor, was no longer predominantly Southern by 1920. National in membership, it would grow in strength thereafter especially in the Middle and the Far West, in states like Indiana and Oregon. It drew to it people who shuddered at the alleged stores of arms stacked in the basements of Catholic churches, who had read in Ford's *Dearborn Independent* of the bearded patriarchs planning the conquest of America. The fiery crosses warned the Under Man. The patriots would act to defend home and country, ride out the stranger, and fight and burn, to make all whole and pure once more.

To ride out the foreigner would be a hard and arduous task. First, it was necessary to shut the long unguarded gates through which the additions to his strength still flowed. The campaign to bring immigration to an end was now at last to come to a successful close.

The old restrictionist forces had by no means been satisfied with the literacy test they had so avidly desired. The measure had no sooner been enacted in 1917 than the Immigration Restriction League began to agitate for more restrictive steps still. The war had not relieved any of the anxieties which had turned Yankees, and Southerners, and organized labor against the newcomers; and the racist xenophobia of the postwar years raised their fears to fever heat.

The literacy test proved no barrier at all. Even the inferior races, if they had to, could learn to read. With the reëstablishment of transatlantic trade, the old tides resumed their course. In 1920, almost a half-million strangers crossed the ocean; a year later the total was well over 800,000. The sore spots of Europe, festering in corrupting disasters, seemed about to discharge their poisonous contents upon America.

In the emergency, there was no time for further debate. At hand was a new scheme proposed by Sidney L. Gulick, a Protestant missionary long active in Japan. In his own work, Gulick had been troubled by the discrepancy between the Christian professions of the brotherhood of humanity and the American policies that labeled Orientals inherently inferior to whites. His formula resolved the discrepancy: to limit all immigration, European as well as Asiatic, in conformity with the percentage of each nationality already in the United States would not discriminate invidiously against the yellow people and yet would actually admit only an infinitesimal number of Chinese and Japanese.

The Johnson Law of 1921 made available to every nationality an immigration quota of 3 per cent of the foreign-born of that nationality resident in the United States in 1910. The Immigration Act of 1924 superseded this provisional measure. For the time being, the quota would fall to 2 per cent and the base year would be 1890. But the Act also elaborated a permanent policy. It rested on the assumption that the character of the American population was unalterably fixed and that its national origins could be ascertained. A statistical examination of the population of the country from the first Jamestown settlers to the last arrival in 1920 would reveal the exact proportions of the various bloods that flowed in America's veins. It would only be necessary to set the quotas in terms of those proportions and the United States would remain ever as it was. Of the 150,000 newcomers each year, every nation outside Asia would have a quota based on the percentage of people derived from it by birth or descent in the total American stock in 1920.

The law which became fully operative in 1929 was thus not simply restrictive, but discriminatory as well; for it recognized a rank list of peoples who could be admitted in the order of desirability with the Nordics at the top and the eastern Europeans at the bottom. Ironically, in view of Gulick's original intentions, it also gratuitously insulted the Japanese by abrogating the old Gentlemen's Agreement and by imposing an absolute interdiction upon all Orientals.

At once, the volume of transatlantic immigration began to contract, declining to below 200,000 by the end of the decade. From among families yet to be reunited there were still handfuls of people willing to wait for visas, willing to accept the rigorous scrutiny by officials under the new law. But the mass movement that for a century had brought millions of Europeans to America was over.

In the long run, it might have drawn to a close in any case. Europe itself was changing. Along the new Soviet frontiers extended an imposing barrier increasingly difficult to cross. Throughout the continent, militaristic regimes held their men to long periods of military service; and in some places land reforms and more orderly systems of health, old age, and unemployment insurance gave potential immigrants a stake in remaining where they were. But American policy was at once decisive. In the countries of western and northern Europe which received the largest quotas, the birth rate had begun to fall and population growth was actually tapering off, while in southern and eastern Europe where the birth rate was still high the quotas were dismally low. Most important, the new policy was an official act of rejection. Few would undertake the difficulties and dangers of the crossing in the face of clear signs that they were not welcome.

From the Western Hemisphere the immigrants were still free to come. As a gesture to the Monroe Doctrine and to Pan-Americanism, Congress had exempted the Americas from the operations of the quota system. The new laws had not applied to the New World; and Canadians and Mexicans, among others, had only to pay the head tax and pass the literacy test to be able to cross the border. Immigration from Canada which had slumped in the decade before 1920 rose rapidly in the ten years thereafter; more than 900,000 British- and French-Canadians, entered the United States.

American officials in the same decade counted less than a half million Mexican immigrants. Those figures were undoubtedly low; not all who crossed this frontier waited to be counted. During the war, the Labor Department had actively recruited Mexicans to work in the Imperial Valley of California, in the beet fields of northeast Colorado, and elsewhere. Although such laborers were imported with the understanding they would return to their homes, many of them escaped official supervision and remained in the United States. Employers, after the war, repeatedly encouraged these cheap, docile hands to cross the border, and sought to exempt them from the head tax, the contract labor law and the literacy law. It became common practice for Mexicans to slip back and forth across the Rio Grande, for more or less extended periods of work in the United States. By 1930 they and their children numbered in the neighborhood of two million.

With an unfailing supply of foreigners no longer available

to man expanding industries the steady internal shift of population reached new high levels. As earlier, the general drift was northward and westward. By the end of the decade well over three million of the thirty-eight million Americans born in the South had moved to the North. Negroes were particularly apt to leave; in 1930 there were almost two and a half million in the northeast and northcentral states. Migration, whether by blacks or whites, was still toward the cities; by now the urban population far outnumbered the rural and over 36,000,000 Americans lived in ninety-three places with more than 100,000 inhabitants. Detroit and Los Angeles had leaped above the million mark, the former by a growth of 56 per cent in the decade, the latter by a spurt of 115 per cent. New York's rate of expansion was by now more sedate; still that city had almost achieved the seven million mark.

While the continued mobility of the period brought its share of attendant unsettlement, an all-encompassing prosperity concealed the difficulties. After a brief postwar depression, the country's productivity and wealth grew phenomenally. By 1925 the National Industrial Conference Board estimated the national wealth at 355 billion dollars, an increase of almost 80 per cent over the prewar level. Almost every branch of the economy thrived — trade, construction, and, above all, industry. The index of manufacturing production rose by 80 per cent between 1921 and 1929, with growth especially impressive in chemicals, metals, and automobiles. Even the shadowy areas had their compensating bright spots. If coal production declined, then aluminum, petroleum, and water power more than made up for it. If agriculture lagged behind, then real estate boomed in Florida, California, and Iowa.

Population also took its familiar upward curve. Between 1920 and 1930 the total increased from one hundred five to one hundred twenty-two million. The heavy immigration of the first few years of the decade had contributed to the increase and the actual rate of growth was lower than in previous years. But whatever the source, that growth was still impressive, larger than in any previous ten year span. There was no cause for lack of confidence here. Indeed, by all the statistical measurements of the past the nation had survived the war and peace with unimpaired energies.

Yet some wounds would not heal. The crisis had brought into question a major assumption as to the nature of American national identity. The wartime demand for loyalty and conformity and the postwar xenophobia had cast a pall of suspicion over all the groups which sprang from some foreign source. The effective end of immigration was accompanied by the implication that those groups ought to fade away and ultimately disappear.

These were not theoretical questions. For many Americans, the war had dislocated the old group life they had known, had cast suspicion on the integrity of their associations and their leaders. The German-Americans suffered most severely; but all those accused of hyphenism bore similar losses to some degree. Other groups, like the Italians and Jews, labored under the imputation of radicalism cast upon them. And, with but two exceptions, all had to begin to cope with new problems created by the end of immigration.

The two exceptions were the French-Canadians and Mexicans, who escaped the last necessity because the flow of newcomers among them continued. The recent arrivals from Quebec strengthened and stabilized the organizations they discovered already in existence, adding to memberships and establishing a link to the source at home. The Mexicans found a less complete associational life at the start, but now helped to develop one. Primarily agricultural workers, who followed the cycle of crops with only a few fixed settlements in California, Texas, and Colorado, they had essentially migratory existences. Still they clung together as other immigrants had. In some places they slipped into the colonies of Hispanos, Negroes, and even German-Russians. But where the number of those permanently settled in a place grew large and stable, they sought each other out, formed mutual aid societies, or joined lodges of the Alianza-Hispano-Americano. In 1927 these organizations were strong enough to act aggressively in their own self-defense. The Federation of Mexican Societies in Los Angeles helped organize the Confederation of Mexican Labor Unions, modeled after the confederation in Mexico. A strike in the Imperial Valley in 1928 was at least partially successful despite the hostility of the sheriff who threatened the Mexicans with deportation.

The growing stability of the Mexicans, nurtured by their contacts across the border, stood in marked contrast to the unsteady situation of other groups which no longer could draw upon their old sources in the same way. Organizations accustomed to recruit new members from among the new immigrants were now cut off from replenishments. The foreign, transoceanic ties of these people grew ever less binding. Yet they did not thereby become like everyone else. What then set them apart?

Their children asked the same question. The second generation generally had passed through the American schools, had perhaps acquired a sense of skepticism as to the European ways they saw at home. But they did not seem thereby to merge into the rest of the population around them for they could not cease to identify themselves with their immigrant parents whose life they shared to some extent. Growing up into the lodges, the churches, the societies, the young people discovered themselves more and more important in the management of affairs, especially as the volume of immigration declined. They had not even a common foreign origin to help them account for these affiliations; after all, they were American-born. Like their fathers, they were driven to wonder, what then set them apart.

An answer was all about them. The war, the peace, and the postwar decade were replete with the definitions of loyalty:

patriotism was the means by which the individual identified himself with his national group. The immigrants and their children found it easy to suppose that nationalism of some sort was at the heart of the ties that held them together. The intensity of nationalist sentiments and the forms that expressed them varied markedly from group to group. That depended upon how they had been affected by the war, by postwar anti-immigrant feeling, and by the quota system. But all were, to some degree, influenced. It was tempting to continue to claim a share in the earliest American past. The pursuit of colonial ancestry was unremitting; and group after group laid claim to Columbus and to the Revolutionary heroes, as if thus to prove themselves worthy, as groups, of a share in American nationality. Yet, for such people the demand that loyalty be 100 per cent was an insuperable obstacle. They had also to explain and justify their antecedents outside the United States. The French-Canadians were not only fond of recalling the contributions of Lafayette and the Acadians; they were also inclined to stress their affinity to French language and literature, just as the Italians dwelt fondly on both Columbus and Dante, the Poles on Kosciuszko and Copernicus, and the Negroes on Crispus Attucks. Paradoxically, this often involved the strengthening of sentimental ties to countries which these Americans had actually never seen.

Within the terms of group life that emerged in the 1920's, however, these ties could not be restricted to purely cultural concerns. On the one hand, in the United States, every group act seemed to involve political nationalism; on the other, the European states labored to influence the rising power of the United States through such ties to American citizens.

Quasi-political movements, therefore, came to absorb a growing share of the attention of all groups. After the First World War Americans were more involved with the affairs of the world outside their continent than ever before, despite the apparent isolationism of the times.

Most impressive were the people who attempted to create completely new overseas states. Thousands of Negroes, detached in Northern cities from their traditional fixed places in Southern society, found a momentary hope of deliverance in Marcus Garvey's promise of a black republic in Africa. Spurred by the Palestine mandate and the Balfour Declaration, American Zionists continued their efforts on behalf of the Jewish settlement there. More Italian-Americans than ever before felt concern about political developments in the homeland; and the delusive imperial dreams of the Fascists who had just come to power offered an attractive escape from the immediate difficulties of American life. In more familiar terms, also, the English-Speaking Union, the Carl Schurz Foundation, and similar organizations continued to strengthen the attachments between various groups of Americans and one nation of Europe or another.

Whatever its form, nationalism was incapable of supplying the actions of these groups with positive meaning. Defensive responses to the frightening developments in American society, these movements revealed a groping uncertainty concerning the future forms of American life. Furthermore, the exacting conceptions of patriotism left by the war brought into question the division of loyalties that seemed involved.

Other efforts to justify separateness and difference in a society that demanded conformity had only limited success. The vision of the melting pot, with its emphasis upon the diversity of the sources of culture lingered on. Yet, despite the casual optimism of *Abie's Irish Rose*, the conception stumbled upon the insistence of many Americans that the culture of the United States was already fixed and defined, not subject to new modifications.

Other Americans rejected the notion of a homogeneous society which swallowed up and digested all the cultures it encountered. The intellectuals especially were determined that their particular cultural heritage not be lost, but survive in a pluralistic society — like the instruments of an orchestra, said Horace Kallen, separate yet capable of playing in harmony.

These ideas had little relevance for the mass of men who lived under the pressure toward a conformity that weakened their communities and deprived their lives of order. For the time being prosperity made the tension tolerable. High wages and the appearance of plenty led them in pursuit of fortune; the other matters were unpleasant, but perhaps would straighten themselves out in the future.

Except on the farms! There disturbing signs of trouble gave unheeded warning of the approaching collapse.

DEPRESSION AND WAR AGAIN

1930–1952

CHAPTER VII

The Impact of Depression

All hopes that a self-contained American America might go its own secure way through a disordered world collapsed as the consequences of depression emerged in the 1930's. The speculative panic of the fall of 1929 led remorselessly to industrial decline in the next three years and to complete economic stagnation through the economy from which there was no recovery for a full decade.

These were more than the reverberations of a fall in the price of stocks. This was the payment for the decade of prosperity in a world that never had recovered from the war. The new debacle began in central Europe where the peace had left a productive system tottering along among the restrictive walls of narrow nationalisms. The collapse then spread westward and to the United States, where the trends of the 1920's had destroyed the power to resist. The long-term slump in agriculture merely continued; and manufacturing felt the effects of loss of purchasing power and of markets. A painful contraction set in, marked by decline in the level of production, by falling national income, and by the rise of unemployment.

At first Americans met the disaster with jaunty confidence. Depressions were, after all, familiar incidents of the past, the usual prelude to splendid recovery. Prosperity lay in wait around some neighboring corner which, once turned, would reveal a chicken in every pot and a shiny new car in every garage. The complacent statements of leaders of government and industry for a time offered soothing reassurance to all but the most skeptical.

The effects of the reassurance wore off with each repeated application. As the indices of production continued to drop, there was less heart in the well-worn phrases. In the rural areas, homeless families on the move were disconcerting evidence of the gravity of the situation. In the industrial cities, the corner apple-sellers and the victims of actual starvation demonstrated that the crisis was certainly one beyond the capacity of charity to relieve.

As 1932 drew to a close, loss of faith chilled the country. There seemed no hope of change in the meaningless mouthings of leaders without plans. Weary of aimless waiting, men saw the respectable institutions of this economy crumble. In town after town, the bronze doors of the bank one morning remained shut and the depositors, yesterday secure, saw the abyss of poverty open before them. Panic gripped the nation as successive investigations revealed the mismanagement and dishonesty of those once mighty in finance. This was not like the past, but rather the end of a whole familiar world. The bank holiday, when it came, brought in its total cessation of business an almost welcome end to a played out era.

The nation welcomed the New Deal in eager anticipation. The parades, expressions of enthusiasm by people who had had little cause for cheerfulness, were a tribute to the fresh spirit in Washington. Now, at least, something would be done. The feverish action of the first hundred days, the signs of planning, effort, and direction encouraged those who had almost lost all hope. The New Deal *élan* would persist through the decade and would survive the various changes of program that marked its course.

The new administration solved some of the problems of the crisis. But it brought no recovery. For six full years after 1933 the depression continued without substantial abatement. Unemployment remained consistently high. Some of the idle were absorbed into work made for them by government spending; others were supported by government relief. But even the restoration of their purchasing power did not bring business back to prosperity. The volume of industrial production did rise in 1936 and 1937 and there was an advance in the price level. But this was achieved by technological improvement rather than by expanded employment. And when government spending fell off, a recession appeared that showed the lack of stability in the economy. If there were any germs of confidence in an economic revival, this recession extirpated them. Only the rearmament program and the start of the war in Europe ultimately lowered the level of unemployment.

The lengthening bread lines, the relief rolls, pulled thin American faith in the future. Opportunity had run out, perhaps back earlier with the close of the frontier, perhaps in some change in the structure of capitalism. Now it was necessary to conserve and plan to use limited resources carefully.

Some social scientists came to believe there were already too many people in the country. The pace of population growth was declining as the birth rate fell everywhere but in the Southeast; and the proportion of people over sixty-five rose from 5.4 per cent in 1930 to 6.9 per cent in 1940. Nevertheless, that any newcomers should be admitted was altogether unthinkable. The flow of immigration ceased entirely. The volume permitted by the quota system was low and economic disaster had deprived the promised land of its attractiveness. In many cases, the quotas were not filled; it was as well to starve or live on the dole in the Old World as the New. But to make absolutely certain that the strangers stayed away, presidential orders in September 1930 instructed consular officials to interpret strictly the clause excluding persons likely to become public charges. The gates were slammed shut. In some years more people left the country than entered it; for the first time, the United States counted a net deficit by migration.

Only in a few parts of the world, in the 1930's, was America still a name to exert a magic attraction. In Mexico, proximity to the border and the ease of drifting across and back, induced a seasonal movement, fluctuating in strength with economic conditions, but adding little to the total permanent population.

Much more important was the growth of immigration from Puerto Rico. This island, when depression came, had been thirty years under American suzerainty; the change in sovereignty had led to many innovations but to few improvements in the standard of living of its depressed residents.

The islanders themselves were sometimes disposed to ascribe their every ill to colonialism and to their political subjugation to the United States. But, though neglect from Washington may have aggravated, it did not create the fundamental unsoundness of Puerto Rico's economy. In this agricultural society, the mass of the people lacked land and the production of restricted staple crops was incapable of supporting a population that kept rising from the pressure of a phenomenal birth rate. The result was widespread poverty. Thousands of laborers without a place on the soil drifted to the cities where neither jobs nor housing waited for them. And, if the population almost doubled between the beginning of the century and 1930, it was despite a frightening annual toll from tuberculosis, hookworm, and infant mortality — the pathological concomitants of pauperism.

In the absence of incentives, a profound inertia settled over the island. By the early 1930's, almost three-quarters of the population were to some degree dependent upon public assistance. The somber melancholia of the men stood out in bleak contrast with the sparkling waters and the lush vegetation around them.

In the more prosperous postwar years, some Puerto Ricans had begun to seek a new life on the mainland. They had gone under contract or worked their way over, taking the marginal places European immigrants no longer filled. Following the routes of trade, they clustered in New York City. In 1930, the Puerto Rican Department of Labor established an employment service in New York to assist the emigrants and thus indirectly stimulated the trend.

The movement accelerated under the impact of the New Deal. The welfare legislation of the 1930's, though weakly administered on the island, discouraged extreme exploitation by local employers. Improved health services lowered the rates of death and disease. The assurance of relief eliminated some of the risk of migration. For perhaps the first time, therefore, the hopelessly depressed glimpsed the vision of opportunity, saw the light of possibility that their efforts might be rewarded by a better life. The number who responded to that challenge mounted year after year. Somewhat more than one hundred thousand had come across by the end of the decade.

The largest concentration was always in New York City. There the newcomers faced an adjustment complicated by their own unreadiness for urban life and by the trying times in which they had arrived. Without any usable skill, they entered the labor market precisely when it had the least need of them. Competing against a mass of unemployed, they accepted the most menial and worst paid jobs. As a result they were as poor in New York as they had been in Puerto Rico.

Poverty distorted their family life. Often women found it easier to secure jobs as domestics than men as factory laborers. Numerous households were divided as the wives came to the States, while the husbands for whom there was no opening remained behind. Or, if both crossed, their relationships were inevitably strained when the woman became the wage earner while the man idled his time away.

In the metropolis, however, these people met other exasperating social problems. A large percentage of the Puerto Rican population was colored; but color on the island had not been the critical social bar that the newcomers discovered it to be on the mainland. They were not able to secure entree to the organized labor unions, except for the Spanish-speaking branches of the cigar makers and the ladies' garment workers. The choice of housing was painfully restricted, for existing residential prejudices operated against the Puerto Ricans as effectively as they did against the Negroes. Crowded together in undesirable neighborhoods on the edge of districts already colored, the immigrants accumulated in slum ghettos. From Harlem across to the East Bronx, they made their homes in dilapidated tenements in which the elements of decency and order were practically impossible to establish. The overcrowded quarters gave them little shelter against the sufferings their strangeness and their color earned them. In the cold-water flats, men, reared in the tropics, were drained of energy, so that tuberculosis and other illnesses took a heavy toll among them. The communities that received them felt their presence in mounting rates of crime, disease, and pauperism.

All social adjustments were slow. The Puerto Ricans were Catholics, culturally remote from the native Negroes, and therefore did not find a place in the existing colored churches. Yet color and differences of language made them alien in the American Catholic parishes and parochial schools. Some found their reading matter in one or another of New York's Spanish newspapers, but communal institutions attracted them hardly at all. Those blessed with complexions light enough to enable them to pass, dropped their affiliations and drifted away from the group, leaving in it mostly the less fortunate who maintained their identification as a means of evading the more general discrimination that overwhelmed the Negroes.

The one other substantial group of newcomers were refugees from Germany. The Nazis were terribly in earnest in their threats to eliminate by extermination or expulsion those not in sympathy with their political ideology and those whose ancestry offended the Aryan notions of racial purity. Emigration began almost at once, gathered force after 1937, with the annexation of Austria and the intensified anti-Semitic campaign that year, and continued to the outbreak of war. Perhaps 80 to 85 per cent of the refugees were Jewish, the rest, political.

A complex of factors reduced the willingness of the United States to receive the newcomers. The conferences at Evian (1938) and Bermuda (1943) proved incapable of contriving an international plan for dealing with the problem; and American isolationism made the task no easier. Depression and the high level of unemployment generated an unwillingness to complicate matters by the addition of even small numbers of newcomers. American Jews, themselves involved with domestic anti-Semitic agitators, were fearful lest the demand for relaxation of the quota laws play into the hands of their enemies. Finally, there was a general reluctance to stir up again the old bitternesses of the early 1920's. As a result, whatever immigration occurred came within the terms of existing laws and of the old quota system.

The new immigrants were different in their social origins from the immigrants of any earlier period, as different as the United States they reached was from that of the nineteenth century. Both the ability to leave Europe and the ability to enter the United States were selective factors. It required capital and resources to escape from Germany and to satisfy the American admissions requirements. Consequently, only a few of the new arrivals were unskilled laborers. Their background, rather, was that of the upper-middle class of central Europe; and their economic, educational, and cultural attainments were of a corresponding level.

The results were reflected in their adjustment. To begin with, they found it more difficult to attain a satisfactory occupational adaptation than had their predecessors. The refugees did not confront the desperate search for work, with starvation the alternative, as did immigrants earlier in the century. But neither were the *émigrés* of the 1930's prepared to settle for menial employment. Naturally, they sought the situations for which their education and training had prepared them. Yet these were precisely the positions most difficult to secure during the great depression.

Restrictive laws that barred some professions to all but citizens accentuated the contraction of opportunities. Thirty-eight states closed the practice of law to aliens, twenty-eight states, that of medicine. Accountancy, pharmacy, dentistry, and teaching were similarly limited, while a few states likewise restricted the licensing of engineers, architects, nurses, barbers, and plumbers. Nor was citizenship an immediate open sesame. Intolerant professional associations and compliant public officials found extralegal means for excluding the competing outsider even after the grant of citizenship made him an American. The result was often a difficult period of preparation before the refugee found his place.

To compensate, their immigration also differed from the earlier in its organized quality. Unlike the old free movement of individuals, this transfer of population was highly circumscribed and carefully regulated by the government of the United States. Furthermore, a number of well-organized voluntary associations stood at hand to aid in the processes of crossing and resettlement. These people, therefore, did not pass through the chaotically tragic voyage of their predecessors. On the contrary, they moved in comfortable accommodations with the way generally planned for them, and with ampler assistance in finding places for themselves in America.

As a result, the possessors of capital or transferable business skills began to make a successful transition quite early, establishing new industries or locating themselves profitably in old ones. Scientists and other academics whose knowledge could pass easily across national frontiers also began to win places in American institutions. Physicians were slower to adjust to the new terms of practice, and the lawyers often found their training totally inapplicable. Of the rest, the majority sought places in the skilled trades and clerical occupations.

The nature of their employment and adjustment tended to

disperse the refugees through the whole nation. Furthermore, the newcomers and the agencies that assisted them were sensitive to the possible criticism of immigrants who clustered in a few cohesive settlements. Consequently, they were widely scattered everywhere in the United States, often in small towns and rural communities. In many parts of the country, the arrival of the strange doctor or chemist first introduced the musical and literary tastes of Berlin and Vienna and established new contacts with European culture.

On the other hand, in the larger cities, and especially in New York, the refugees were numerous enough to develop an associational life after the older pattern. They joined together in mutual-aid societies, founded religious and educational institutions, and supported newspapers and cultural organizations. These supplied the means of self-expression and assisted the immigrants in their adaptation to the new life. Yet expulsion from Germany had cost them their homes and cut them off, against their will, from a world they loved. *Bei uns*, they would often say, identifying themselves with the old land in comparison with the new. Many refugees, decisively shaken, long remained insecure, suspended between two worlds.

Quantitatively, neither the German refugees nor the American immigrants from North America influenced the country's population substantially in the 1930's. Indeed, in this decade, movement across the border was less significant than that within the boundaries of the United States.

The westward movement in America had by no means come to a close. Its form, however, had changed.

The Pacific coast was now the goal. Shortly after the First World War, California had its second discovery. In the decade before 1930 its population leaped by 65 per cent; in the decade after, by 21 per cent more. The movie industry, fabulously thriving, attracted some newcomers, the expanding agriculture of the southern parts of the state, others. The mild climate also pulled away from less attractive corners of the country increasing numbers of retired men and women with the leisure to pursue sun and health.

Florida passed through a simultaneous boom. The coastal resorts, at first places of refuge for the wealthy and fashionable, were laid open to the masses by the railroad and automobile. A dizzy speculative development led into a spectacular real estate collapse in the 1920's; but the state's population in that decade nevertheless soared by more than 50 per cent. And in the ten years after 1930, it continued to grow at a rate only slightly lower.

These movements, however, bore little resemblance to the earlier advances on the American frontier. They led not to the settler's cabin on the cleared plot, but to the stuccoed towns and cities, suddenly sprung up at the ocean's edge. Under the clear sun, against the slow tempo of near-tropical conditions, disjointed societies took form unlike any theretofore found in the United States. They held more than their share of old and idle people, for whom stability and security were almost total ends and who therefore felt themselves always in imminent danger. Everyone was a stranger, seeking without much success to strike roots and to establish orderly patterns of life. The very communities lacked continuity with the past; the sprouting towns seemed to come from nowhere. Although in California societies proliferated — of New Englanders, of Iowans, and of the sons of the pioneers — they could not give those who sought it a sense of being at home. Uneasiness pervaded even their great raucous annual picnics and their members remained open to many forms of eccentricity; every fad of religion, of health, of politics was attractive.

Such people were particularly resentful of newcomers of still another sort who came to California in these years. Those who sought the comforts of retirement or the glamor of the movie lot were unwilling neighbors of the fugitives of the disasters that overwhelmed the Great Plains after 1933. That region, brought under intensive cultivation almost fifty years earlier, now suffered from a succession of calamities that set in motion a large part of its population. From the Dakotas south through Oklahoma and Texas, an ill prepared agricultural system now reeled under a succession of blows. Droughts and winds took the top soil away from once fertile farming states; and the "black blizzard" of May 1934, created a great dust bowl within which no plant could grow. Too many farmers here had optimistically extended themselves during the war and now looked debt in the face; too many were tenants without hope of paying rent. Flight was the only recourse. There was no place for them in the small farms of the settled East. But in the golden West, they heard, jobs could be had on the great fruit and grain lands. A procession of battered automobiles between 1935 and 1939 carried fully three hundred and fifty thousand farm families from the dust bowl to the Pacific coast.

The arrival of the "Okies" was a mixed blessing. Willing to work at any wages and under any conditions, they relieved employers of dependence upon Mexican and other foreign hands. But these migratory laborers were burdens upon the communities into which they came. Perennially dependent and poorly housed, they became a threat to health and relief budgets. Drifting about, their children could not profit from education; and the group remained a disturbing unassimilated element in the whole society. Yet these were American citizens, old stock Anglo-Saxons in the main, who could not be rejected as "foreign," and only desperate quasi-legal measures limited their flow across the borders of the Pacific coast states. The Farm Security Administration and other New Deal agencies made feeble efforts to ameliorate their condition. But in 1939, they were still an undigested mass without a fixed place in the region.

Elsewhere migratory agricultural labor followed better

established patterns. The spread of large-scale cotton farming to the Southwest depended on Mexican pickers. Mexicans, with Filipinos, harvested the nation's sugar beets, as the Portuguese did the cranberries of New England, and Italians and Negroes the vegetables of New Jersey. Poorly paid and intermittently employed, these people led a marginal existence, on the move from the Rio Grande to Michigan, from Florida to Maine. In the 1930's the factories of the field rather than of the city presented America its most ominous human problem.

Only in the South did the growth of cities in these years approach the pace of earlier decades. The steel and textile towns of Alabama, Virginia, and North Carolina continued to gain in population. Power supplied by the Tennessee Valley Authority opened another region to manufacturing; and the Gulf cities in Texas, Louisiana, and southern Alabama expanded on the basis of petroleum and its derivative chemical industries. Such centers drew thousands of tenant farmers and sharecroppers who no longer saw the possibility of making a go of it on their eroded and exhausted soil.

For the Negroes the flight was still northward. The Agricultural Adjustment Act and the contraction of cotton production had squeezed out the marginal sharecroppers. Opportunities were scarce for black men everywhere; but in Harlem or Bronzeville there was freedom and some hope. A number of white "arkies" and "hilligans" also continued to go north to Detroit and the other manufacturing cities which had in the previous decade eagerly sought their labor.

Despite these additions, the long-term rise in urban population was coming to a halt. For the first time, there were signs of reverse migration back from the cities to the farms. The estimate in 1935 that there were almost two million Americans in the countryside who had not been there five years earlier may have exaggerated the extent to which that represented an actual return to rural living. The trend was nevertheless significant. Largely these were fugitives from the depression, people who had sought their fortunes in the cities and failed, and who now returned to family homesteads; for although these were already "fished-out ponds," the security they offered, poor as it was, was preferable to the unlimited risks of life in the towns.

For many Americans the risks of city life outweighed the attractions. Increasingly, those whom jobs held in offices and factories nevertheless sought also to escape in their residences. The image of the small town, the homogeneous community of neighbors, now was transmuted into that of the suburb with its array of trim houses and green spaces unsullied by the dirt, the crime, the alien people of the city. The drift toward the periphery of the great metropolitan districts continued, accelerated by the influence of the automobile. In the nature of the case, the well-to-do found it easier to commute than the poor; but as the population dispersed, families at almost every social and economic level could find suburban security somewhere in their urban borderland. In 1940, perhaps one-third of the residents of the nation's 140 metropolitan districts lived in such peripheral areas.

By contrast with those of earlier eras, the shifts of population in the 1930's were motivated less by the will to grasp new opportunities than by the desire to minimize risks. These were signs of a disturbance that would affect also many other aspects of the life of the decade. The shock of prolonged depression, coming before Americans had fully recovered from the disturbances of the First World War, evoked a painful longing for security and stability.

Men now were prepared to throw themselves into any movement, no matter how extravagant, that promised relief from the unbearable failures to which the times condemned them. The enthusiasm for the New Deal in the spring and summer of 1933 had some such revivalistic elements in it. The winter before, Technocracy, Howard Scott's scheme for an economy of push-button efficiency, enjoyed a brief vogue. By 1934 Upton Sinclair's *I, Governor of California*, a simple formula for socialism, had sold a million copies; and his EPIC (End Poverty in California) party came close to winning the gubernatorial election that year. Another proposal, "Thirty dollars every Thursday," with "Ham and eggs" for the unemployed almost won the state election of 1938.

Every panacea was able to mobilize substantial support. Huey Long's slogan, "Every man a king," had made him governor of Louisiana, and senator by the time assassination cut short his career. In 1936, Dr. Francis E. Townsend claimed to have led 6,000,000 members into the movement for an old age revolving pension fund that would pay out $200 a month to those over sixty. At the same time Father Coughlin's National Union for Social Justice urged upon millions of adherents a radical program that included nationalization of credit, utilities, and natural resources. So, too, hundreds of Americans, intrigued by descriptions of the planned society of the Soviet Union, found it possible to work, on domestic questions, with Communists, who for reasons of their own were then pursuing the policy of the United Front.

All these chaotic strivings for a magic solution to the nation's ills were doomed to failure. The depression continued its inexorable course until the end of the decade. Unemployment persisted also, and with it a grinding pressure on every social institution.

Few men could bear the strain of these tensions without the consolation of some explanation for the disastrous, unsteadying changes. Yet, fewer still were willing to find the fault in America itself; the buoyant optimism and sense of confidence with which Americans had in the past always thought of themselves made them reluctant to think that. Whence, then, had the evil flowed?

Often before, it had been easy to see in the erratic disruptions of life the insidious hand of the foreigner. The

Know-Nothings, the A.P.A., the Klan, had thus achieved a fleeting notoriety. Now, the immigrant was no longer a prominent figure. But in the lingering shadows of the great war and the unhappy peace some unseen, alien enemy still lurked.

The isolationism of the 1920's had not divorced America from the world's perplexing problems. Relationships to the League and to the World Court continued to inflame men's tempers. Father Coughlin turned against the New Deal when President Roosevelt proposed that the United States become a member of the World Court. Shortly thereafter the Spanish Civil War summoned up bitterly conflicting loyalties. The initial response, sympathy for a republican government that replaced the decrepit monarchy and corrupt dictatorship, persisted among many groups, while increasingly Catholic support in the United States went to Generalissimo Franco, self-proclaimed defender of the faith against the atheistic radicals. At the same time the rise of Fascism in Germany and Italy troubled numerous Americans sentimentally attached to those countries. And the long debate over neutrality policy embittered every aspect of the nation's foreign relations.

With the source of so many difficulties foreign, some Americans now again discerned international conspiracies to subvert the Republic. Vestiges of anti-Catholic feeling lingered from the 1920's. The Klan, the contested Democratic nomination of 1924, and the presidential campaign of 1928, had stirred up ugly passions that still smoldered. In the rural Middle West, in the South, and in suburban communities in California and New York, scattered bands of Klansmen continued to frighten themselves with the image of the Pope.

The Jews were now the more prominent target, however. The Protocols of Zion and Henry Ford's naïve charges of twelve years earlier were no longer taken seriously; but they had planted in the consciousness of many Americans the stereotype of the international Jew, equally threatening whether as banker or revolutionary. And, through the 1930's, successive social irritants endowed the figure of the Jew with a sinister aspect.

As the second generation grew more numerous and as the immigrants adapted themselves to American conditions, they moved out of the constricting ghettos and occupations into which, for want of alternative, they had drifted on arrival. More conspicuously than ever before, Jews sought entree to the respectable professional and white-collar employments; and they longed, as others did, for the suburban escape from the hardships of urban life. On both scores they encountered hostility. The depression had limited professional and clerical opportunities so that there was less room for outsiders; and by their very presence, the Jews — strangers — destroyed the cozy sense of familiar sameness that was the reason for being of the suburb. An ugly complex of discriminatory practices had taken form by the mid-thirties; it limited the number of Jews admitted to professional schools, excluded them from favored positions, and by gentlemen's agreements barred them from desirable residential quarters. Such practices evoked resentment both from the Jews who suffered and from the prejudiced who profited. The Jews saw their portion of America unjustly withheld; and the others labored under the need for convincing themselves that the practices from which they profited were somehow not — as they seemed to be — counter to their own belief in equal opportunities.

Sparks from Germany touched off these materials for anti-Semitism. Conscious that persecution of the Jews had outraged opinion in many parts of the world, Hitler created an international apparatus for the National Socialist Party in order to justify his actions through a vigorous propaganda campaign. That campaign extended to the United States both through official agencies of the German government and through unofficial channels sponsored and subsidized by it. A single theme echoed through the blatant oratory and the lurid pamphlets: the Jews, racially impure, were engaged in a conspiracy for world domination and must be fought by any available means.

A flurry of activity followed. Anti-Semitism began to play a part in the programs of a wide array of organizations. Among the most important in the rural South and West were George Christian's White Shirts and William Dudley Pelley's Silver Shirts. In the industrial cities, on the other hand, Fritz Kuhn's German-American Bund attracted a large following. Toward the end of the decade also many followers of Father Coughlin fell into the ranks of the Christian Front as the radio priest espoused the theory of a conspiracy against the Republic by the international Jewish bankers.

The young men who joined these movements had stood about idly on the street corners, without purpose or direction in their lives. Unrewarding jobs, or lack of jobs, had matched the emptiness of all social experience for them; they had not known where they belonged or with whom to identify themselves. Then, through the fog of fears and uncertainties, they perceived the menacing figure from without — alien, unknown, and potentially dangerous — the source of all that threatened their security. At least to discover the hidden cause was comforting. And in the murky halls, the orators brought back courage; a sense of resolution came from being together; and recognition of a common foe brought them unity and direction.

As these organizations multiplied in the 1930's, they seemed on the verge of making their influence decisive in American life. However, they never became more than reservoirs for the emotions of frustration and the tensions dammed up by the depression. The channels had not been opened through which those emotions might pour to transform the society.

Despite their mounting numbers, the shirted movements

did not become significant political forces. Scattered and disunited, they nowhere attained more than temporary local control. In 1936, the followers of Father Coughlin had joined the disgruntled remnants of Midwestern agrarian insurgency behind the candidacy of William Lemke for the presidency. But the vote cast for the Union Party had been tiny, had not in the least impeded the Roosevelt landslide. The campaign showed only that some wider organization was necessary to draw these groups together, before they could exert any determining effect upon American politics.

Yet no such comprehensive organization of the hateful and the violent emerged. Occasional efforts in that direction ended only in failures. The most carefully planned attempt to arrive at some common front came in 1937 in Philadelphia at a great convention presided over by General Van Horn Mosely. This well organized and well financed meeting, however, could not evolve a workable program to unite its participants. Although Pelley, Coughlin, and the others held each their own following until the end of the decade, they achieved no basis for effective coöperation. Millions of Americans enlisted in these ranks for greater or lesser periods, but the years went by and the angry emotions of the marching men ebbed away in endless oratory.

In part, the vanity and ambition of the rival chieftains were responsible for the chaotic inability to organize. Each saw himself a leader, held his own cherished image of a place at the fore, and refused to accept second place to anyone.

But more positive factors condemned these movements to futility. Their members joined up but they hesitated at the brink of action. There was relief of a sort in reading the bombastic newspaper or listening to the haranguing speech. But powerful restraints kept these Americans from translating their violent thoughts into action.

The example of Hitler and the evidences of the ravages of Fascism in Europe were themselves terrifying. Through the decade the loose phrases of the anti-Semitic agitators acquired an even more portentous meaning, as Americans came to see across the Atlantic what consequences would follow. As Mussolini moved along in Hitler's train he disabused those inclined to self-deception. Totalitarianism was unlimited. To accept a part of it was to step toward the full fatal plunge; and only the conscious fascists wished that.

The mass of followers in both the proto-fascist and utopian movements had not rejected their heritage of humanitarianism. In their own confused way, many of the dissident movements attached scraps of liberal doctrine to their own programs. Huey Long and Father Coughlin, for instance, through part of their careers actively supported President Roosevelt and the New Deal; and their ultimate change of line did not immediately dissolve the liberal loyalties of their memberships. "Ham and eggs," the Townsend Plan, Social Justice, and the other economic and social panaceas held each a devoted body of supporters. But, to such signers of petitions, social security and minimum wage laws were of a piece with their own favorite nostrums. The successive New Deal measures, therefore, seemed partial victories. The devotees of Townsend and Coughlin did not lose the hope that effective change might come through legislation, and they continued to vote for Roosevelt. Faith in politics prevented them from accepting the tactics of direct action. At the same time, the New Deal wrapped up the very laws they sought in broader liberal arguments about equality and the rights of the common man.

It was highly significant that in the New Deal were involved attitudes altogether contradictory to those purveyed by the would-be American *führers*. The New Deal had drawn together a political coalition of diverse groups who saw in it the opportunity for satisfaction of long-standing social grievances. The members of some of these groups suffered from discrimination, yet they believed that action by the government could relieve them of part of the burden of prejudice. For them, the New Deal was to be the instrument of social as well as economic reform.

Among these groups were such Catholics as the Irish, the Italians, and the Poles; the great majority of American Jews; and the Negroes becoming newly conscious politically. This coalition, first tested in the election of 1928, four years later supported the New Deal in full strength. It was encouraged in its aspirations by the President and by the important figures in the administration dedicated to the ideals of diversity and equality as elements of the liberal heritage.

The groups that thus became aware of the political goals of social equality often referred to themselves as minorities. They did not thereby acknowledge they were literally less than half the population; together, indeed, they were probably a majority. In the use of the term they meant rather that they were underprivileged, discriminated against in the opportunity to strive for the economic and social rewards of American life. Their immediate objective was elimination of the prejudices that held them down on account of their "race, religion, or national origin."

That some of these people themselves became involved in nationalistic or fascist movements, that some of them bore prejudices against others, was evidence of the contradiction in their own position. Nevertheless, the hope of reform by the New Deal kept alive their liberal affiliations, and stood in the way of any total involvement with the Pelleys and their like. To that extent, the ideal of a diverse yet equal America still was attractive.

Perhaps another consideration — more basic still — lay behind the failure of the proto-fascist movements. Every attempt to draw together those scattered organizations revealed the contradiction in their very nature. Hostility to some alien group gave form and purpose to their membership. But there was no consistency to the shape of the enemy that each discerned. What the Black Legion feared was not what excited the Christian Front. And every effort at collaboration collapsed at once because the very first encounter, as likely as not, uncovered a hidden foe in the would-be friend. Trapped by their own fears and hatreds, the men who drifted toward these movements could not escape the heritage of their own diverse origins.

These movements, therefore, brought no sustained relief from the strains of depression. They supplied no answers either to the concrete question of how to lead a life of minimal decency in a disordered world or to the more general question of what were the terms of identification around which men could furnish a basis for a satisfying group life. During the same decade, other Americans, under the same pressures explored alternative solutions to those problems. The impulse toward nationalism led the searchers for security to particular group affiliations as well as to 100 per cent Americanism.

CHAPTER VIII

New Patterns of Action

The profoundly unsettling effects of depression extended to every existing group in American life. The old
forms were rarely adequate to the new necessities. Contraction of opportunities challenged the assumption that American society would continue indefinitely fluid, with room
for every variety of person, free to organize his life in whatever associations he wished. The unprecedented need for
making choices in these matters inevitably curtailed the scope
of all voluntary endeavors.

This need was the product of more limited resources, but
also of the form in which American society met the crisis.
Under the pressure of falling incomes, private schools and
hospitals, mutual assistance societies, and cultural and social
organizations with small membership found it difficult to
make ends meet, at the very time when demands upon them
were greater than ever before. With expenditures high and
receipts low, these agencies faced the danger of collapse.
Large-scale integration of efforts seemed the only saving step.

Tentative attempts at federation had already pointed the
way. In a number of cities, since 1895, the Jewish philanthropic societies had joined in annual combined fund raising
appeals. In Denver and Cleveland there were early endeavors
to achieve the same result on a more general level, taking in all
welfare agencies without regard to ethnic affiliations. By
1932, community chests existed in some four hundred cities.

The next decade deepened the urgency. The total number of federations grew by almost 50 per cent. More important, the functions of the federations started to change. From simple devices designed to gather contributions, they began to turn into policy-making organizations that advised their constituent agencies upon planning, efficiency, scope of operations, program, and personnel. Although the individual organizations within the federation retained their autonomy, dependence upon the fund raisers for allocations severely circumscribed their freedom to act.

This development coincided with another that radically altered the nature of philanthropic and cultural associations. The growing complexity of their services and the demands they made on technical efficiency transferred their administration from the hands of the devoted amateur to those of professional experts. The society now was less likely to be constituted, financed, and directed by those who expected to be served by it, and more likely to be supported by community funds, managed by impersonal, trained administrators, and outside the control of those it assisted. The effectiveness of its work undoubtedly gained by the transformation. But in the process, it lost a good deal of its function as an association drawing together like groups as participants.

At the same time, the voluntary associations met unprecedented competition from those under state auspices. The New Deal viewed relief, broadly construed, as a matter of direct concern to the federal government; through the Federal Emergency Relief Administration and other agencies, through unemployment benefits, and ultimately through social security it made available sums of money far beyond the command of private charity.

Increasingly, then, men in need looked to the state rather than to associations they themselves had formed. But the state was impersonal and not free to recognize group differences among those it served. As its functions broadened, the sphere left to voluntary organizations contracted. In the process, one of the basic modes of American group action atrophied.

The other activities that had once given form to the ethnic group also fell into disuse. The newspapers, the theaters, the schools that once supplied it with channels of expression still had vitality in the 1920's. As late as 1927 the formation of a national Alliance of Polish Literary Dramatic Circles of America showed the extent to which such interests persisted. But the rise of mass media, incomparably greater in resources, deprived the more limited ethnic organs of their utility.

Hearst and Pulitzer, conscious of the potential reading public in the second generation, had begun the process. The picture tabloid in the 1920's completed it. In the next decade every newspaper that served a limited group found it difficult to make ends meet. The subscription lists of the Brahmins' *Boston Transcript* and of the foreign language press alike plummeted rapidly. The number of journals declined; and those that survived more frequently now found it possible to hold on only as weeklies or monthlies supplementary to general newspapers.

Before 1917, the theater had already suffered from the effects of vaudeville, which in its heterogeneity appealed to a wider level of tastes. The movies, particularly with sound added, and then the radio, completed the disintegration of the older institutions. In a few places, the theater, professional and amateur, persisted; and occasionally there were Italian or Jewish or Polish "hours" on the radio. But all such survivals were exceptional to the tendecy to address the most general public without reference to the peculiarities of the groups within it.

The profound consequences of these changes emerged slowly. The man who had established his residence where he could, who through choice and necessity had joined a coöperative society for security against illness, death, and destitution, who had found expressions of his own culture among a vast variety of available journals and theaters, such a man had seen the meaning of his affiliations in the numerous functions the group served. That meaning was lost when he was assigned a place to live from a housing project list, was guarded by a number on the social security rolls, and was supplied entertainment mostly through the anonymous and unresponsive mass media. Even when the old organizations persisted, their function was gone.

People who moved still tried the older ways; as strangers, the Puerto Ricans, the refugees, the "Okies" could not at once fall in with the populace around them. But the new associations they now formed often competed in function with the state and were less likely to hold the loyalty of their members.

Only in those rural regions, better endowed in resources to withstand the full impact of depression, was the disruptive influence successfully resisted. In the older Northwest — Ohio, Indiana, Illinois — and in the Gulf region of the South, entrenched farmers weathered the effects of falling prices and stubbornly held to the old forms as if to compensate by their own excess of conservatism for the changes in the rest of the world about them.

Everywhere else change was irresistible; not even the pretense of stability remained. Some of the oldest self-contained communities in the nation dramatically collapsed. The decade of the 1930's witnessed the total abandonment of the effort to maintain the standard of an exclusive society. The good old families, the Brahmins in Boston, the Knickerbockers in New York, the Main Line clans of Philadelphia, now surrendered the claim to dictate tastes and establish values. The great town houses were boarded up or torn down, for there were no longer the resources thus to preserve social difference from the less wellborn. Good works no longer justified the dinner dance; the impersonal government bureaucrat had taken the place of Lady Bountiful as guardian of the welfare of the grateful poor.

These groups suffered also from the responsibility for the great depression. Dominance over the Republican Party had given them political power, control of the great financial institutions, economic power; and the end of their use of power had been the great collapse. When Charles Mitchell, once president of The National City Bank, began to serve his jail sentence, he discredited these groups as leaders in the eyes of the nation; at the same time, he drained away their own faith in themselves. Too confused to protest, the mighty J. P. Morgan permitted a press agent to hand him a midget at a Congressional committee hearing. The old gentlemen who fumed in their clubs at the traitor to his class in the White House nevertheless dared to sponsor no practical alternative. Meanwhile, the very clubs had fallen upon hard times, and opened their doors to outsiders, just as the exclusive schools, under the pressure of the urgent need for tuition fees, became less selective about the antecedents of the families of their students.

The young people in these groups now coming to maturity found the old pretensions altogether irrelevant. In the wild 1920's, their faith in the family verities was shaken; now they were, likely as not, marrying outside the old closed circles, or even accepting positions in New Deal agencies. Increasingly they wandered off into the outland regions, and lost their identity in a wider Yankee society; by the same token newcomers from the hinterland more often than before found themselves accepted by the good families who were no longer capable of maintaining their distinctiveness.

Comparable dislocations occurred everywhere. Those who had identified themselves through immigration suffered the impact not only of depression, but of restriction. The total halt to immigration after 1924 severed their last remaining ties to the Old World. Without additions from across the ocean, memories of transatlantic antecedents faded. As the second, and, in time the third, generation grew to maturity, affiliations based upon some remote immigrant ancestor became ever less meaningful. The old language and the old customs grew unfamiliar in the bustle of American life; and that further sapped the vitality of the old societies. Why, the young people asked, should they pay premiums to the mutual aid society rather than the insurance company? Their elders increasingly found an answer hard to come by.

The larger groups showed some capacity for survival; but the smaller ones struggled painfully against the inclination to dissolve the old affiliations. The Chinatowns lost population; the Albanians began to find religious and linguistic ties with the Greeks; and others sought also some meaningful adjustment.

All these people did not, however, merge anonymously into some homogeneous mass. The variety of their origins and the diversity of their adjustments perpetuated differences among them. In 1940, still, young men born in America would refer to themselves as Polish or Italian, without knowing at all the language or country with which they thus identified themselves.

Such differences survived, but not as the result of adherence to any theory of American life. Intellectual speculations concerning the merits of assimilation proved irrelevant. The differences neither disappeared nor remained the same. The orators still paraded the virtues of 100 per cent Americanism; but often enough the ranks that turned out on "I am an American" day marched behind the varied banners that symbolized their separateness. There was no evidence here for the assumption that uniformity would be the end result of Americanization — whether by assimilation or by the operations of the melting pot. Yet at the same time, the fact that many yielded to the pressure of Americanization ran counter to the conceptions of cultural pluralists who had hoped that the old groups could survive unchanged. In a society characterized by rapid change, former lines of identification and affiliation became blurred as the conditions that had originally defined them disappeared. But new associations emerged from the impact of the forces that reordered the United States in these turbulent years.

The course of world events since 1917 had conspired to persuade Americans that the most relevant terms of group identification were those of nationality. The 1930's emphasized that tendency and furthermore narrowed the conception. In the decade of fascism, rearmament, and impending wars, the romantic notions of a cultural fatherland became anachronistic. Nationalism now, more than in the earlier decade, meant patriotic loyalty to a political state and the symbols of its power — flag, hymn, armed forces, and soil.

The demands of nationalism were trying for American Jews who could not attach these emotions to an existing state of their own. Nevertheless, the tragic circumstances that now confronted them in this decade pushed Zionism into the forefront of their group life.

The movement had grown steadily but unspectacularly through the 1920's, stimulated by the Balfour Declaration and by the resolute course of Jewish settlement in Palestine. Only a small minority of Jews in the United States were actively affiliated with Zionism, although the desire to preserve the nucleus of pioneers in the Holy Land drew a much wider body of support. The American Jewish Congress, dominated by Zionists under the leadership of Stephen S. Wise, actively labored to sustain the Jewish homeland; and through the Jewish Agency, even those who objected to the political ideals of Zionism contributed to the maintenance of the cultural and social institutions in Palestine.

The decisive turning point in the history of the movement came in 1933 with Hitler's accession to power in Germany, an event which had immediately significant repercussions. It created in a very troubling way both practical problems of relief and psychological problems of security.

As victims of religious and racial persecution, the German Jews made an instantaneous appeal to the conscience and sensibilities of their coreligionists in the New World. Yet the recently adopted American immigration laws made it unlikely that many refugees from Hitlerism would find homes in the United States. Nor was any other country eager to open its doors to such newcomers. Regardless of ideological considerations, therefore, it was argued that only in Palestine were a substantial number of Jewish *émigrés* likely to find shelter.

Furthermore, the terrifying spectacle of the effects of Nazism raised the fear that Jews were nowhere secure. The brutalities were, in themselves, shocking enough. But that they should occur in Germany, once the most enlightened nation of Europe, was altogether disheartening. The simultaneous development of fascist movements with anti-Semitic overtones in Great Britain and in the United States gave credence to the Zionist argument that Jews could be safe only in a homeland of their own. Growing numbers of American Jews now began to take an interest in the Zionist movement.

The ultimate implications of Zionism for American Jews were still unclear. Few took the trouble to wonder whether or not creation of a homeland would end Jewish life elsewhere in a total migration back to Palestine. The immediate necessity was to support the actual migration of refugees to Palestine. Yet British policy, based upon friendship for the Arabs, stood in the way. A bitter struggle to compel the English government to admit more Jews to the Holy Land lasted until 1939; the White Paper that year finally frustrated these hopes by prohibiting all further settlement.

British intransigence heightened the nationalism of those American Jews who were totally committed to Zionism. With this object lesson, they hammered away at the non-Zionist aim that the "homeland" might be simply a place of refuge with the Jews permanently a minority. The inability to secure relief under the British mandate seemed to show that only an independent, sovereign nation could provide homes for the fugitives from anti-Semitism. Thereafter there was no middle ground; most American Jews disregarded ideology and supported Zionism as the only feasible means of offering a refuge to the Nazi victims.

Hitler's grasp of power also reshaped the organizational life of the German-Americans. For them the First World War had been a shattering experience. They had suffered from the wartime condemnation of Kultur, and had been disappointed in peace. Through the 1920's their associations remained weak, disorganized, and suspect. The Germans, however, had gained in numbers through immigration in that decade for, perversely, the quota system gave the former enemies of the United States a larger share of places than almost any other group. The newcomers were the disappointed men of postwar Germany, many veterans, many nationalists, some National Socialists; they confirmed the sense of betrayal and defeat among those already here.

The Nazis made capital of these confused emotions. Goering advised all Germans living abroad to "remain in your hostland, a granite rock of Germandom"; and the Party early established branches in the United States, as it had among groups of *Auslands-deutsche* elsewhere. National Socialists were thus active in the first national congress of Americans of German stock, in New York in 1932. The year following saw the formation of the Society of Friends of New Germany, of its journal, *Das neue Deutschland*, and of an organized body of stormtroopers, the O-D men. Thereafter Nazi influences intruded ever more forcefully into the organized life of German-Americans.

At the start, the old, respectable elements among the German-Americans disapproved; the Bundists complained they were "too American." But the capacity to resist ebbed away.

Disorganized by the depression, some German-Americans, like some other Americans, were tempted by fascism. Furthermore, the influence of the German government and of the Nazi party apparatus was strong, in finances, in fanatical leadership, and in propaganda that capitalized upon sentimental attachments to the homeland. Finally, the Jews, who had once been active in German-American organizations, now withdrew and left the field open to anti-Semitic agitators. Indeed, the organized boycotts of the Nazis and of Germany under Jewish and liberal auspices consolidated the support of German-Americans behind the American Nazis.

Some strongholds of opposition remained. But by 1934, such pillars of the old German America as the Steuben Society were giving reluctant support to the Bundists. Others, like the Ritter family and its newspaper, the *Staatszeitung*, were neutralized and ineffective. The German-Americans failed to halt the efforts of the Nazis to take command. The American branch of the National Socialist Party therefore grew in strength and influence, despite the indictment and flight of its first leader, Heinz Spanknoebel. In April 1936, it became the German-American Volksbund under Fritz Kuhn. An active program of parades, publications, and camps mobilized its members and kept the nationalist fervor of its following at a white heat. The riots it precipitated in White Plains and Yorkville, New York, in 1938 demonstrated its power.

By then, however, the Bund's position vis-à-vis the American government had deteriorated. After Munich, the administration was increasingly hostile to Hitler's regime, and the position of any group that was openly sympathetic to the Germans became less tenable. Investigated by Congressional committees and the Federal Bureau of Investigation, the Bund lost the support of many German-Americans, fearful of another such period of persecution as they had suffered during the First World War. The Carl Schurz Foundation founded the *German-American Review* to counteract the influence of the

Nazis; the German-American League of Culture fought them, and ultimately even the Steuben Society and the Ritter family joined the attack. But a hard core of devotees remained faithful to the Bund, proclaiming their patriotism and justifying their allegiance by working arrangements with 100 per cent American fascists like Pelley.

The consequences of nationalistic affiliations were less clear for Italian-Americans. Mussolini's early efforts to plant centers of fascist influence in their organizations had achieved some success by 1930. After that date respectable opposition collapsed. The Italian-Americans had never had strong leadership; neither the church nor labor organizations had offered room for development. The mass of immigrants remained without trustworthy guides to critical American issues, particularly after the Sacco-Vanzetti case discredited the old radicals. Apathetic, the Italians were inclined to evade decisive stands.

Mussolini attracted them by his forcefulness and by his ability to gain the "respect" of the "Anglo-Saxon" Americans. The Concordat of 1929 also gained him the approval of the Catholic Church in Italy and in America and removed the last suspicion that he was somehow radical or unorthodox. At a time when the Italian community was least self-confident about its place in the United States it was cheering to find a man "who does not let a fly pass his nose," who could face up to the powerful ones of the earth and have his way.[1] The prosperous building contractors and small businessmen watched "the big wop" on the balcony with admiration and wondered whether Fascism was not also the way of winning respect for the Italians in America. Stimulated by scholarships, free trips to Italy, and financial aid, organized opinion in the group, in its societies and newspapers, steadily veered to Il Duce's support. Only a handful of die-hard radicals held out on ideological grounds.

The commitment to Fascism as the desirable form of government for Italy, although not for the United States, was fixed by the time of the Ethiopian War. Widespread condemnation of Italy in the United States did not weaken, but rather consolidated, Italian-American support for Il Duce, who had "led the nation back to the reality of life . . . by . . . his eminently spiritual doctrine" and "by molding into action the Fascist intentions." [2] American and British criticism was but Anglo-Saxon hypocrisy and discrimination against Italy. The Spanish War further strengthened the link to Fascism, now wearing the mantle of champion of civilization against Communism.

Analogous impulses permeated the life of other groups as well. The unification and independence of Poland stimulated Polish-American nationalism. Factional disputes had enlivened the history of the Polish National Alliance and the Polish Falcons (Sokoli) in the 1920's, but their concerns now more frequently focused on relationships to the old homeland. The Polish Student Association of America and the Kosciuszko Foundation devoted themselves to the task of planting in the native-born generations a knowledge of the ancestral language and national culture.

So, too, Irish-Americans were not content with Home Rule, but nurtured grievances with regard to partition; the Hungarians found themselves defenders of the Horthy regime; and the various peoples who looked back to central and eastern Europe maintained in an intensified form the nationalist aspirations of the postwar period.

While these sentiments were phrased in terms of some foreign tie, they originated in America. They expressed a submerged discontent with the disheartening conditions of the 1930's. Nationalism thus was an outlet for the grievances of some Puerto Ricans who drifted into a number of organizations that struggled for the independence of the island. Even the Mexicans in the Southwest were drawn in the same direction; the Unión Nacional Sinarquista had branches with substantial membership in several American cities.

The strength of these currents was most graphically illustrated by their pull upon Negro Americans. Back in the 1920's, the Garvey movement had shown the potentialities of such developments. The will of the Negroes to find some national basis for their identification sprang from the same factors as in other groups. A multitude of leagues and alliances attempted to organize their desire to stand by each other. The same impulse went into campaigns to induce colored people to shop in Negro stores and to give jobs to Negroes, and led to the Harlem riot of 1935. The desire for some kind of black political loyalty resulted in a strong attachment to the Negro states. American colored men watched events in Haiti and Liberia with interest throughout the decade and the outbreak of the Italo-Ethiopian War in 1935 aroused them to spirited action. The conquest by whites of one of the few independent Negro nations came as a shock. "Ethiopia has become the spiritual fatherland of Negroes throughout the world," proclaimed *Opportunity*.[3] Everywhere, it pointed out, "peoples of African descent have been stirred to unparalleled unity of thought." The offer of Hubert F. Julian, Harlem's flamboyant Black Eagle, to be Ethiopia's air force was not an isolated or eccentric gesture. The action represented a deep emotional response from a black man who wished to see himself in the same nationalistic terms as other men.

The significance of such chaotic and contradictory impulses lies in the needs that called them into being. These sentiments and deeds were not rejections of America, but the efforts of confused people to explain their place in it. The very men who thrilled to the slogans of Zionism or responded to the appeal of Mussolini were also members of the Jewish or Catholic War Veterans and of the American Legion.

These were thus bewildered attempts, under the new circumstances, to account for themselves as they were.

The Indians were not capable of making the same choices
as other Americans, yet were affected by analogous forces.
Still not completely free, they found, as earlier, that the
crucial decisions were made for them by the dominant whites.
Nevertheless, for the red men too the decade was one of
changing emphasis, for those decisions were shaped by the
nationalistic assumptions now current through the whole
society.

Ever since the passage of the Dawes Act the American
government had assumed that Indian tribal organization would
disintegrate, that the Indian lands would be dispersed among
the individual owners, and that the Indians would ultimately
be amalgamated with the rest of the American population.
The policy had never been successful; its results were pauperism of the red men, who deeded away some ninety million
acres of their land between 1887 and 1934. Vigorous protests
in the 1920's had produced some results, but the decisive
alteration of policy came under the New Deal.

The turn in Indian policy was the product of the humanitarian impulses injected into the Department of the Interior
with the Roosevelt administration. There was still a concerted
effort to improve the condition of these wards of the government. But the prevailing assumption now was that the Indians
would fare best under the traditional tribal forms rather than
by assimilating into the dominant streams of American life.
Romantic conceptions of the Indians, the interest of anthropologists in Indian culture, and a heightened awareness of
factors of nationality, all contributed to the formulation of
the new attitude.

The Wheeler-Howard Act of 1934, passed with the assistance of Secretary of the Interior Ickes and his adviser, John
Collier, gave form to the new principles. Thereafter the
tribes that chose to do so could preserve their reservations

and manage their property as corporate entities. The landless could acquire new holdings and a revolving fund for government loans gave the Indians the means for resisting economic pressure to sell. Special provisions in 1936 and 1938 extended similar benefits to the Oklahoma Indians. These measures gave the tribes the power to prevent the dissolution of their holdings and thus to preserve the traditional organization. By the end of the decade, well over half the tribes in the country had come under their terms. The impetus had come from outside, but in time the Indians themselves were interested and some of them began to dream of an Indian nationalism of their own, within which preservation of their language and culture would preserve the differences between them and other Americans.

The nationalism to which so many Americans turned in the 1930's had steadily gained strength since the First World War. Economic insecurity was now an additional stimulus to the will for some kind of loyalty. Whether nationalism was expressed in one of the "native" movements that emphasized 100 per cent Americanism or whether it took the form of some effort to stress the identity of a particular "national" group, it offered momentary relief from the tensions of depression. By affording a means of identification with a group, it gave the individual some reassurance that he was not altogether alone in the face of unprecedented problems. In the solidarity of the anthem ringing out, in the comfort of repeated tradition was a basis of security.

Yet few Americans, even those who fled to the closed circle of the *bund* or order, would consciously surrender their more general identification as equal members of American society. Often while they insisted that they were different from the "others," they also affirmed that they were somehow the same and deserved to be treated on an equal footing. The groups that had been subjects of discrimination and prejudice were not merely driven to a consolatory nationalism. At the same time, they were determined to defend their rights as Americans.

Defense organizations, like nationalistic ones, therefore, sprouted through the decade. The Catholics had not yet recovered from the attacks upon them in the 1920's. Furthermore, the Spanish Civil War and the issues of European politics divided them from the liberals who had stood by their side in 1924 and 1928. More than ever it seemed necessary that they act vigorously on their own behalf. Organizations such as the Knights of Columbus and the Paulist Fathers continued their work of apologetics although more aggressively than earlier. Overt signs of anti-Catholicism diminished through the 1930's, yet the group remained alert.

Among Jews, the necessity of defense seemed acute. The American Jewish Committee founded toward the beginning of the century to protect Jewish rights in all parts of the world now became most heavily preoccupied with anti-Semitism in the United States. The Anti-Defamation League established during the First World War set itself the task of eliminating educational, economic, and social discrimination. The American Jewish Congress took as its sphere of activity the achievement of equal rights through law and social action. And the Jewish Labor Committee united some union strongholds toward similar ends. These diverse agencies reflected the very deep ideological and social divisions among American Jews. Various efforts to unify these organizations or to allocate functions among them ended uniformly in failure.

The cleavages among Negroes also persisted through the decade. The Urban League and the National Association for the Advancement of Colored People found their activities overlapping. Yet past disagreements and continuing differences between the two associations kept the memberships apart.

Meanwhile, other colored men found their own means of defense. Hardest hit by the depression and most painfully

the victims of discrimination, the Negroes in the Northern
cities grasped at every ray of hope. Now Major Devine, a
revivalist who had come out of the South to preach on Long
Island, New York, moved to Harlem and became Father
Divine. His following grew steadily in size, attracted at first
by a scheme of economic coöperation that seemed miracu-
lously to abolish want, but then held in absolute devotion by
the simple denial that color existed. In the hymn addressed to
those who had created the iniquitous barriers of segregation,
Father Divine told the prejudiced:

> If you live on the face of this earth from now on,
> You are going to enact the Bill of Rights;
> You are going to sit side by side with the one
> You spurned in your arrogance and selfish might.
>
> You will see that each has the same hopes and desires,
> The same ambitions, the same thoughts — the same
>   prayers as you;
> You will see each living soul has a heart just like yours —
> That is, if GOD lets you live to see it through.[4]

The day Father Divine's angels dreamed of had not yet
come. But Negro defensive efforts were better rewarded than
in the past. A new political situation, the product of the great
northward migration, now bore fruit. In the Northern cities
the Negroes were voters, often holding the balance of power.
They were part of the coalition that elected the Democratic
Party in 1932. Thereafter they began to reap their share of
the rewards; their will could no longer be disregarded in
national or local politics. For the time being, the opposition
of the Southerners set limits to the advances. But in 1938, the
Gaines Case established the basis from which the Negroes
could destroy the practice of segregation in education, and
other precedents began to undermine the whole Jim Crow
system.

The defense organizations worked on behalf of large groups of the population, but the numbers that participated directly in their activities were small. Wider support for these efforts came through more general political means. Since the rights involved were those of all Americans, all men who suffered from prejudice and discrimination could participate in a common struggle.

The New Deal offered a platform on which all the "minorities" could stand together. Its vague ideology of the common man emphasized equal rights, and it depended for political support on groups that looked to government action for remedies to their disabilities. Furthermore, Jews, Negroes, Irishmen, and Italians were more prominent now than ever before behind official desks and created an atmosphere sympathetic to the aspirations of the "minorities."

Actually, before 1941, the federal government took no direct action to correct the inequities among groups of Americans. But the New Dealers hoped to attain the same ends indirectly. All the evils of prejudice and discrimination, they argued, had their roots in economic exploitation. Therefore, the elimination of poverty and the furtherance of social justice would in themselves cure all the tributary maladjustments. High wages and slum clearance were the means toward abolition of group hatred, as of juvenile delinquency and of other forms of social pathology.

New Deal strategy assigned to the unions an important tactical role. The assumption was that these organizations were in the forefront of the fight on behalf of the exploited elements; every gain for labor, therefore, appeared a step forward for the underprivileged. Furthermore, conceivably the unions could drawn into their ranks workers of every background and, by creating an identity of interests, secure equality of conditions for them all.

The actual development of labor organization reinforced these ideas. As the C.I.O. split off from the A.F.L. and invaded the mass industries, it enlisted the unorganized laborers in steel, automobiles, and other branches of manufacturing. Among the new members were numerous immigrants and the sons of immigrants and not a few Negroes, people who had theretofore been excluded from the ranks of organized labor. For these people, the unions were more than agencies of collective bargaining. They were social, cultural, and fraternal associations as well. Sometimes membership lines coincided with those of the ethnic group. But often continued mobility made it difficult to maintain that relationship. Thus the International Ladies' Garment Workers Union had emerged from the First World War largely an organization of Jewish laborers. By 1937, fully 100,000 of its 250,000 members were Italians, and before the decade was over, it accommodated also a rising number of Puerto Ricans. In either case it was possible to regard the union as the instrument of defense of group rights through the furtherance of economic reform.

Communists seized upon the disposition to view all issues as surface reflections of economic problems. This was their opportunity to attract the support of the minorities. The idea of capitalizing upon national differences was not new to the Party and the distress of the underprivileged promised a rich harvest of recruits. In the 1920's the Communists had attempted to filter into the labor movement; during the depression they redoubled their efforts.

The lures were various. The Soviet Union was held up as a model society in which economic reform had totally obliterated race prejudice. Party members were ostentatious in demonstrating their egalitarianism, pushed Negroes and the members of other minority groups into positions of prominence, and rushed to the fore in such incidents as the Scottsboro Case. While thus insisting that all men were the same, they nevertheless encouraged nationality differences, issuing their publications in several languages, setting up the

International Workers Order in distinct nationality sections, and paying lip service to the notion of an autonomous Negro republic.

Furthermore, the policy of the United Front after 1935 did not release the Party from all its ideological fetters, but did enable it to work out a rationalization for coöperation with non-Communists. It could then claim that all non-fascists should draw together against the single common enemy and that Communists were only the most left-wing, the most militant, of many allies engaged in a struggle for the identical ends. Communism was proclaimed twentieth-century Americanism and, under the pressure of the crisis of the 1930's, not a few individuals were willing to work with it on those terms.

None of these expedients gained the Party a substantial following, however. The committed Communists had few ties to the organized life of American society. The avowed members, like W. Z. Foster or Earl Browder, Benjamin Gitlow or Whittaker Chambers, were men estranged from their own antecedents and from the activities and associations in which their fellow citizens were involved. The very alienation that made these people rebels prevented them from influencing the associations and the cultural media which guided the thoughts and the actions of most Americans.

Occasionally, unions in the battle against stubbornly intransigent employers, as in the automobile and electrical industries, accepted the aid of the Communists or of one of their fronts. Now and again a politician or some national organization, in the struggle over some particular issue, also used these willing workers. But that rarely led to any deeper commitment. The well-established labor unions and voluntary associations had their own leadership capable of resisting infiltration. In this decade, therefore, the Party was more often used than capable of using other Americans toward its own ends.

Furthermore, the Party's line, handed down from outside,

was a persistent impediment. Too often its disruptive tactics showed up its ulterior motives. At critical moments, some permutation in the party policy, as in 1939, forced upon it an abrupt and embarrassing shift of line that caused defections. Most important, the Party could not destroy the belief that the goals of the minorities could be attained in other ways without sacrifice of the stake in America that all these groups were increasingly sure they had. The rock upon which Communism foundered was the certainty that defense of equal rights was possible within American society.

The bitter group hostility during the prolonged depression of the 1930's drove men to the defensive. These activities were essentially negative, defined by the assaults of outsiders. Those under attack were in no position to choose their grounds, but were compelled to protect themselves by any means at hand. Rarely could they attempt a positive definition of what they stood for; they fought mostly because their enemies were against them.

In a larger sense this was the problem of all Americans. As the depression proved unyielding to every remedy, as Ethiopia, Spain, and Munich showed the world was plunging toward destruction, an immense yearning for security welled up through the land. To guard the essential rights and values was as much as anyone could hope for. Cautiously men drew together to defend what they had.

The minorities, most vulnerable of all, felt the pressure most intensely. For them, the struggle against prejudice, like the nationalism of the period, supplied a kind of relief from the unbearable tensions of these years of distress.

CHAPTER IX

A Decade of Global War

In September 1939, the long slope down toward war finally led over the precipice. The global struggle that followed dominated the next decade. The United States was from the first involved, neutral though aiding the Allies. The necessities of the conflict quickly transformed many features of American life. All the problems of the people were thereafter framed in a totally new context.

Well before Pearl Harbor, the United States began to feel the effects of the war to come. After 1938 the rearmament program set in motion an economic revival that gathered speed with the hastening sense of crisis after Munich; actual hostilities brought with them a flood of war orders that strained the capacity of factories long idle. Thereafter the level of productivity expanded steadily. Lend-lease and the increase in size of the armed forces spurred the munitions and aviation industries to unprecedented achievements; 50,000 planes seemed an idle vision one year, and became a commonplace the next. The war itself was the climax. The purchasing power of workers newly employed revived demands dormant for many years and stimulated a gigantic outpouring of goods in every branch of civilian economy. Peace did not reverse the trend. There was this time no significant postwar recession. The volume of employment rose with scarcely an interruption through the 1940's.

The requirements of war production and technical innovations altered the configuration of American industry. The Pacific coast boomed on a scale that outdid its earlier advances; the region thrived as steel and aircraft and shipbuilding establishments built up an elaborate manufacturing complex. Along the Gulf of Mexico and in the Southwest, the petrochemical and aircraft industries grew phenomenally; and in the older South, places like Birmingham and the TVA area added steadily to their plant. The development in the Northeast and the Middle West was less spectacular but nevertheless offered a heartening contrast with the depressed conditions of the 1930's.

Prosperity spread to every economic group. The farmers saw all the ills of the interwar period disappear; and businessmen, no longer worried about profits, had only the size of their taxes to consider. The depression had found a swift and efficacious cure.

Long troubled by an excess of labor, employers suddenly faced disconcerting shortages of manpower. The draft drew away substantial numbers at the same time that continued expansion created the need for more hands. Industrial workers now occupied a highly favorable situation. There was a continuous rise in rates of pay and, with the elimination of unemployment, of annual wages. Women drifted back to the factories, and not simply to the marginal light tasks of the past. In the national emergency Rosie the Riveter held down a man's job on the assembly line, and drew down a man's wages. In consequence, family incomes shot swiftly upward.

The restrictive immigration policies of the past were now an expensive luxury. War production occasionally suffered from want of hands to tend the machines or harvest the crops. Employers, in their own way, also suffered as wage rates zoomed out of recognition. Yet the old prejudices were too strong to permit repeal or modification of the immigration quota laws. Whatever adjustments were made were temporary and did not touch the principles of the permanent legislation. Indeed, the McCarran-Walter Immigration and Naturalization Act of 1952 would later perpetuate the old provisions in a more rigid and less tolerant form. Embodying the anachronistic prejudices of the past rather than any estimate of national interests and ideals, that measure would make it still more difficult to deal with the manpower problems already pressing during the war. Meanwhile, unwillingness to depart from the restrictive permanent policy led to a variety of expedients to cope with the national needs.

The first expedient was the regular use of migrants from the Western Hemisphere to whom the quota provisions did not apply. In the Southwest, politically powerful farm, railroad, and mining interests had earlier worked out schemes for the import of Mexicans under annual contract. Now, under agreements negotiated by the two governments, the flow of such laborers back and forth across the border increased rapidly, amounting to well over 60,000 in 1944. The United States government appropriated substantial sums to assist and stimulate this movement. Similar arrangements permitted the entry of Canadian woodcutters and West Indian agricultural workers. The earlier stream of Puerto Rican migrants continued and was accelerated later in the 1940's by cheap air transportation.

The advantages to the employers were clear. The disciplined gangs were brought in when they were needed and shipped out when their usefulness ended, without the opportunity to fix themselves permanently in the United States. But the migrants often resented the attitude that they were good enough to work seasonally only in gangs, herded about under supervision from place to place. They preferred to make their own arrangements and frequently sought to slip back over the border illegally. The number of such surreptitious entries by "wetbacks" mounted steadily. Although no accurate data are available, some agencies estimated in 1950 that there were a million in the country.

The labor shortage destroyed one of the conventional arguments against immigration, that there was no room. The deficiency of workers persisted after the end of the fighting and raised anew the question of whether newcomers ought not again to be welcomed.

The end of the war and the restoration of transatlantic shipping brought a resumption of European immigration from the nations fortunate enough to have sizable quotas. Favorable economic conditions in the United States after 1946 attracted substantial numbers of Germans, English, and Irish newcomers. In addition the ability of the American G.I.'s to make friends everywhere in Europe and in Japan produced a very large crop of war marriages; with the assistance of a special law that cleared their way, some 120,000 spouses crossed the oceans between 1946 and 1952.

The most disturbing debate arose over the effort to make an exception of another class of applicants. The nation now faced a decision as to whether it should take any responsibility for the millions of displaced persons left homeless by the war. Before the fighting ended, there were indications of the vast dimensions of the problem; and the United States had participated in several international conferences to plan a constructive approach. All these efforts had come to nothing, primarily because the restrictive legislation of the past prevented American negotiators from making any commitments on behalf of their government.

Yet this was inescapably an American problem. Indirectly the United States contributed to the support of the displaced through occupation charges in Germany, through the United Nations Relief and Rehabilitation Agency, and through the International Refugee Organization. The nation had a substantial interest in the restoration of European stability; and that could not be achieved without some provision for the millions of men and women who passed their days without hope in the camps of central Europe. Pressure for an emergency act to permit the entry of a limited number therefore mounted steadily.

A stubborn bloc of rural senators deferred action until 1948 when the Displaced Persons Act at last provided for the admission of some 400,000 newcomers in the next four years. The limitations and controls were rigid. But sympathetic administration of the law and the devoted efforts of American voluntary agencies made a success of it.

In the decade of the 1940's, immigration from all sources had added almost a million to the population of the United States. The number was small in comparison with that of the period before 1924, but large in comparison with the 1930's when there were occasional years in which more people left than entered the country. This was a notable departure from the restrictive attitudes of the fifteen years before the war.

The trend away from restriction was indicative of renewed expansion throughout American society. Growth in population more than kept pace with growth in the economy. After 1939 the marriage rate turned upward; in 1941 it was 12.6 per thousand, the highest in history, and it showed no signs of falling. The birth rate entered upon a parallel climb, to the surprise of demographers. Since the mortality rate from all causes dropped in the same years and the number of aged persons continued to increase, the decade witnessed a rapid rise of population. The census of 1950 counted fully 150,-697,000 Americans. The increase continued thereafter at an estimated rate of some three million a year.

The over-all figures gave only an approximate impression of the magnitude of the growth, which was not evenly distributed throughout the nation. Some metropolitan districts like those of Houston and Los Angeles almost doubled in size; and in the plains of Texas or the hills of Tennessee substantial cities housed thousands of residents where there had been only open fields ten years earlier. People in rapid movement had hardly had the time in 1950 to settle down and take stock of the dimensions of the change.

The war and postwar prosperity had abruptly cut across the trends of the preceding two decades and had transformed the economic conditions under which Americans lived. There were still problems and the haunting memory of the depression did not die, but there was also a renewal of the expansiveness that persistently stimulated the productive system.

These changes meshed into a more general social transformation after 1941. Expansion created new opportunities everywhere and released the tensions that had earlier oppressed men in competition for limited places. Meanwhile, the emergency and the patriotic sentiments the war generated dissolved the most acute group antagonisms. The animosities of the 1930's now lost their acerbity.

In the period of neutrality there had been signs in plenty of bitter discord. Some German, Italian, and native fascists were openly sympathetic to the Hitlerite alliance. A larger body of opinion, from a variety of viewpoints, insisted that the United States remain completely neutral in the conflict.

As in an earlier war the core of opposition to foreign involvements was the Midwest, confirmed in its desire for peace by revelation of some of the hidden factors in the decision of 1917. Scandinavian-Americans were inclined in the same direction even after Norway itself had become involved. Significant German-American, Hungarian-American, and Italian-American factions agitated in favor of the Axis. And many Irish-Americans, distrustful of Roosevelt's intention, suspected he was but a cat's-paw to save an empire for the British. These groups furnished the supporters of the America First movement and occasionally became tools of unscrupulous anti-Semitic and fascist agitators. Through the election of 1940, the strength of such elements compelled the President to act with caution and to disclaim belligerent intentions. Incongruously, in this period, the permutations of Party policy led the Communists to collaborate with these groups and in the process to lose the sympathy of most liberals who had been the allies of the United Front years.

For the liberals and many other Americans believed that Fascism was a threat to the whole world. Some were drawn to that opinion by liberal convictions and by the experience of the earlier decades, others by ties of antecedents or birth to the invaded countries. Cultural and personal connections with England were as strong as in 1917 and led some to the opinion that union or close collaboration with Britain was essential to security. To Jews, the first target of Nazism, an Allied victory was the only hope for the survival of Europe. Polish-Americans from the start recognized defeat of Germany was essential to restoration of the divided republic. And successive invasions drew to their side the Dutch, the Czechs, the Yugoslavs, and the Chinese.

The declaration of war resolved all these divisions of opinion. The attack on Pearl Harbor was so openly aggressive, there was no hesitation to the support given the government. The most reluctant elements of the population sensed the importance of the fateful measure and freely subordinated all particular loyalties to the demands of their American allegiance. The Communists too found themselves patriots once more. With the rupture of the Nazi-Soviet pact, the Party line brought them over to support of the war effort, and the government accepted their aid out of the desire to emphasize the unity of all the allied peoples in the struggle against the Axis powers.

The wholehearted response and the absence of disloyalty were not evoked by fear or constraint; the government now did not resort to the restrictive controls and the blatant domestic propaganda of the First World War. The German-

Americans were not maltreated and there was no particular revulsion against German culture. Nor did the Italian-Americans suffer. In 1941, there were fully six hundred thousand Italian enemy aliens in the country and many of them had been openly sympathetic to Mussolini. Yet only two hundred were interned and the group caused no trouble. On Columbus Day 1942, they were relieved of the burdens of their enemy status and thereafter suffered under no disabilities.

Only the Japanese-Americans met another fate. Pearl Harbor was the signal long attended by the racists on the Pacific coast. In the 1920's and 1930's the adjustment of the Orientals had been favorable and peaceful and had created a living refutation of the primitive racial libels spread by bigoted politicians and grasping competitors. Now there was an excuse for crushing the Japanese-Americans.

There followed the most shameful episode in recent American history. In January 1942, the Pacific coast delegations in Congress, under Senator Hiram Johnson, determined to press for the mass evacuation of the 100,000 Japanese as a threat to the nation. A month later the Tolan Committee offered a forum for the purveyors of hate. The Hearst newspapers took up the clamor. General J. L. DeWitt, the cynical and prejudiced commander of the area, yielded to these pressures. Pleading military necessity — which did not exist — he recommended mass evacuation of the Japanese. By the summer the removal had been effected; thousands of American citizens thus lost their freedom and were confined to concentration camps.

The Japanese were more vulnerable than the Germans or Italians; few in numbers and highly concentrated, they could readily be evacuated. But they suffered mostly because of their color; as Attorney General Earl Warren of California pointed out, only the loyalty of Caucasians could be trusted. And the pusillanimous refusal of the majority of the Supreme

Court to overrule the drastic invasion of rights drew also upon racial arguments.

Yet there was a quick revulsion. Not indeed on the Pacific coast where hatred for the "Japs" became enshrined as an article of faith, but everywhere else. Liberal opinion mobilized to support them; and the federal relocation authority assisted them sympathetically to restore their broken lives. Most of all, they themselves, by their patience and continued loyalty, demonstrated the difference between the quality of their Americanism and that of their persecutors.

Vestigial racist sentiments also entered into the three great riots of the tense war years. In the cities, swollen with unfamiliar new residents, strangers jostled each other on the job and competed for scarce living space. Soldiers and sailors on the loose drifted about in search of something to do; and adolescents, bored with job or school, crammed their minds with images of violence out of the newspapers, the movies, or comic books. In the background of the overcrowded slum districts, a motley underworld crowd lived on the edge of criminality.

These were the elements. In New York, Los Angeles, or Detroit, there were often evenings in the hot summer of a day without work when the air was tense with expectancy. Rumors filtered through the bars or around the street corners where the boys waited to hear the baseball scores. Tempers were short; and fancied slights or the recollection of a grievance or a momentary frustration pushed men to the breaking point. Usually nothing happened or at most a brawl spread down the block until the police appeared.

In 1943, something did happen — three times. Petty quarrels got out of hand. Excitement kindled the flames of hatred, and emotion burned throughout the city. Men and boys ran, not knowing where, but driven by rumor in search of some recognizable enemy. Shots rang in the dark, and the battered victims left trails of blood in their flight. Whites fought blacks and Mexicans in Los Angeles, in Detroit, and in Harlem.

These were results no American wanted. Men might differ on the subjects of equal rights and segregation, but none could approve the outbreaks of disorder. The show of violence was too reminiscent of the enemy they fought in Europe and in Asia. Cathartic shame at the outbreaks mingled with determination that they be not repeated. The communities affected entered upon a patient course of remedial action and successfully labored to prevent a recurrence of these disorders. The years after 1945 would not see the long succession of riots that blemished the years after 1918.

Consciousness of the goals for which they fought also hastened the process by which Americans effaced the established patterns of discrimination. The urgency of winning over the people of Asia and Africa made it hard to justify racial inequities at home; and the "minorities," advancing steadily in power and status, were in a position to demand equality of treatment. That ideal was far from attained in 1950, but there had been immense progress toward it.

Civic and political disabilities disappeared almost entirely. In 1941, the Negroes alone were victims in this regard, and they now moved forcefully in their own defense. The N.A.A.C.P. was vigilant, and growing political power gave the group an effective instrument of self-protection. Lynching all but disappeared; the number of colored officeholders mounted; and Negro participation in elections increased. In 1944, the Supreme Court held in *Smith* v. *Allwright* that the white primary was unconstitutional and thus pulled down the barrier that had excluded blacks from Southern politics. In some places, the poll tax and extralegal sanctions still served the same end, but the trend toward political equality was not halted.

Political power was the means by which discrimination in employment was fought. As opportunities expanded after

1939, the resentment of the Negroes at the disadvantages foisted on them mounted. In 1941, A. Philip Randolph organized a march on Washington to demand action by the government, a step which forced a decision by the President. An executive order created a Fair Employment Practices Commission to secure equality of treatment in firms engaged in defense contracts.

The F.E.P.C. was not totally effective; in the South colored men did not get to work side by side with whites. But the measure was nevertheless immensely important. It created a standard to which it was increasingly embarrassing not to conform; and in the North it opened to Negroes a wide range of jobs theretofore closed to them.

Furthermore, it offered a model for even broader laws in the interests of all underprivileged groups. Permanent state fair employment acts in New York, Massachusetts, Rhode Island, and Wisconsin forbade every type of discrimination on the basis of race, religion, or national origin. These laws were not panaceas curing all ills. But they did establish useful criteria of conduct. The advertisements for white Protestants disappeared from the press, and the members of minorities had their first chance at many desirable professional and clerical jobs.

The same principle in a number of states forbade educational institutions to discriminate. As a result the quotas that had often limited the admission of Jews, Negroes, and Italians tended to disappear. Meanwhile successive tests in the courts whittled away at the doctrine of "separate but equal," and opened to Negroes in the South the possibility of admission to public universities and professional schools.

The practices of social segregation did not yield to the same pressure, except where they touched upon public concerns in which the government could intervene. In the South the Jim Crow patterns remained largely unchanged. Many Northern communities recognized residential restrictions, although the courts would no longer enforce "gentlemen's agreements." Hotels, clubs, and resorts everywhere still used their "private" character to exclude Negroes, Jews, and other "minorities." During the war some U.S.O. clubs found it unnecessary to practice segregation, but the armed forces kept blacks and whites apart until the end of the war. It took persistent agitation after 1945 finally to secure the integration of colored and white men in the same fighting units.

Until 1945, the fear would not down that these gains were the results of the war crisis only. "Pray God, the war doesn't end soon," the Negroes were saying. Yet when the rest of the decade consolidated and extended those gains, it was clear that more general forces were at work. Some disabilities had survived. But the racist conceptions were dead.[1]

The movements dedicated to racial and religious hatred disintegrated. The relics of the Klan vanished and the fascist organizations of the 1930's fell apart, tainted by disloyalty and by connections with the enemy. The cumbrous attempt to prosecute the leaders for conspiracy was unsuccessful, but they were nonetheless off the scene by 1945. And the Columbians who tried after the war to stir up the old agitation met swift, ignominious failure. No substantial movement thereafter openly preached the doctrines of racism. When segregation was defended now, it was in other terms — the utility of preserving tradition and the gradualism of progress. Forthright anti-Semitism, anti-Catholicism, and Negro hatred were now the province of the unheeded crackpots.

Before the decade was over, demagogues as unscrupulous as any in American history had begun to spread other kinds of fear. But significantly they meticulously avoided attacks on the "minorities" and rather sought to win them over. Indeed, McCarran, McCarthy, Cohn and the like were themselves but a generation removed from the persecuted groups; and every well-equipped staff required a Catholic, a Jew, or a Negro in its entourage to demonstrate its freedom from prejudice. That was an indication of the extent to which the position of the "minorities" had been transformed.

The growth of tolerance was the product of several factors. The war and the nature of the enemy exposed the true character of prejudice. Few Americans remained un-moved at the spectacle of the gas chambers to which racism had led the Germans. There were few compensations for the sacrifices of war, and those mostly embodied in the hopes attached to the slogan of the Four Freedoms; the logic of that slogan had meaning at home as well as abroad.

Continuing prosperity also contributed to the more relaxed attitudes. High wages and economic security removed the fear of competition and eased the strains depression had caused. Meanwhile the practical gains of the earlier decade were exerting a cumulative effect; as Negroes, Jews, and Italians found places in public offices, in jobs, in schools, and in hotels where they had not previously been known, famil-iarity rubbed away the fright at the strangeness and dissipated the prejudice born of ignorance.

Furthermore, the experience of the war years had been instructive. The boys had shared the same barracks, the men the same workbench; and strangers away from their homes had come to be neighbors. With all the distrust of the initial approach to one another and despite occasional conflicts, they had come to know they need not fear each other. To-gether they had passed through a great trial, and the danger was not yet over.

And this was most important of all, that the danger was not yet over. Properly speaking there was no postwar. Before the Japanese had surrendered, the atom bomb had revealed its awesome power; from the moment it brought destruction to Hiroshima, a frightening shadow reached across the future. Before the boys could come home, Potsdam had revealed the gulf between Russian ambitions and American aspirations;

thereafter successive incidents made clear the threat of this other totalitarianism. At mid-century the war still blazed, now on the battlefields of Korea.

This time there was no place to hide. It was futile to think of escape from the weight of global responsibilities when the wings of man brought America within striking reach of transoceanic enemies. Isolationism was dead, replaced by a sullen, angry nationalism, suspicious of hidden foes and afraid.

There was no time for illusions, for belief in an easy tomorrow into which the dangerous problems would peacefully recede. The country stoically accepted the task of continued armament, the successive crises in the remote corners of the earth, and the ever larger potentialities for destruction. Every family came to live with the possibility its sons would some day crouch in the mud of a distant battlefield. The grim obligations were in somber contrast to the tinsel prosperity of the home front.

This was, therefore, a time for men to cultivate their own gardens. If the major social forces were beyond an individual's control, it was better he should devote his energy to the areas of life he could still shape to his will. The veterans, or those on the way to being veterans, lusted after the domestic virtues. Their dreams were of stability, of the ranch-type bungalow and the family car and the play of children in suburban yards. The little houses splashed in the thousands across the countryside sheltered the men turning inward in the quest for peace of mind.

Threats to back-fence security lifted their hearts in fear and anger. Although every objective measure showed prosperity more widely diffused than before, it all seemed to hang by a thread. In fascinated horror, Americans learned of the conspiracies to rob them of respectability, by the Mafia and the racketeers, by the Reds and the subversives. The same concern with personal stability left housing the most important remaining source of tension in group relationships.

The Black Legion outbreaks in Detroit and the Cicero incident near Chicago exploded out of the intensity of emotions of people who wished to preserve unchanged an appropriate little setting for their lives.

American life did not, however, facilitate the strengthening of roots. Constant mobility had left a mark that could not readily be cast off; these people had moved too much and from too many different places to be able all at once to find their proper niches. Will it or not, they all remained to some degree strangers, removed from their families and the friends and scenes of childhood. To the personal problems of greatest import they found it most difficult to know the solutions. No grandmothers advised them how to raise the children or set standards for the young folk. No accepted communal traditions gave the right answers to the grown people's questions as to the etiquette of personal behavior. Often in the trailer camps, in the housing projects, in the sprawling suburban developments, or in the clumps of newcomers wedged in among the old residents of the Eastern cities, these perplexities spoiled the taste of economic and social gains and left an air of troubled insecurity.

Not many media of American culture could supply guides to the perplexed. Millions of people, sitting in identical rooms, watched the flickering screens and saw the impersonal images directed at no one of them. Fantasies of nightmare violence and idyllic domesticity held their attention but answered none of the burning questions of their lives.

They were not after all the shapeless integers of an homogeneous mass. They desired a sense of identity that would explain why they were different from "One Man's Family." They wished to belong to a group. To be, with their children, a meaningful part of the succession of generations would give a purpose to their striving, supply it with the security of a source and a goal. From the richness and diversity of its social life, America offered them the possibility of choices.

For some now religion became the focal point of ethnic affiliation. Men were not drawn back to the churches by the attractiveness of theological doctrine, however; the trend toward secularism in ideas was not reversed. Some hoped to find in religion a traditional source of authority and discipline. Others looked to faith for a universal psychiatry supplying easy relief for the tensions of a disorderly world.

But the most powerful magnet was the round of practices and the social connections capable of giving order to life in American society. Through its institutions, the church supplied a place where children came to learn who they were, where the right boys met the right girls, where men and women in their groups found satisfying diversion. In this respect, all the sects were now Americanized, their activities set within the concerns of this world and offering their communicants not so much a remote salvation as immediate peace of mind or soul.

The churches were in a strategic position. Religious differences, above all others, were accepted by Americans. Constitutional provisions set this whole area off from the action of the state; and a long tradition of tolerance supported the right to freedom of affiliation. Furthermore, government action in these years encouraged the trend. Some states, through "released time" and similar programs, actively stimulated religious education; and public busses and free lunches supported it.

Religious identifications however rested not on the acceptance of defined articles of faith, but on social choices shaped by ethnic antecedents. Creedal differences still divided Americans into more than two hundred and fifty distinct sects. But those differences now faded in importance. Increasingly religious activities fell into a fundamental tripartite division that had begun to take form earlier in the century. Men were Catholics, Protestants, or Jews, categories based less on theological than on social distinctions. In creed, the High-

Church Anglican and Unitarian were more remote from one
another than the former was from the Catholic or the latter
from the Reform Jew. Yet in many communities the Uni-
tarians and the Anglicans could look back to common antecedents and found themselves joined in a common institutional
life. They regarded themselves as together Protestant, separate from the Catholics and Jews who had other kinds of
grandparents and were involved in other societies.

Significant impulses sustained the development of the three
major groupings. The emergence of national religious coun-
cils between 1905 and 1915 had been largely along these
lines. In the two wars, the government had imposed that
identification upon the armed forces. And the growing tendency to define the boundaries of marriage and intermarriage
within religious terms led to acceptance of the same distinction. The children of Italians were still most likely to marry
the children of other Italians. But when they did not, their
spouses were more likely to be Irish or Polish Catholics than
Protestants. So too, Polish Jews wished their offspring to
marry within the circle of landsmen, but in time were recon-
ciled to have them go off with the sons or daughters of
Galician or Syrian Jews, rather than with Gentiles.

The trend was neither complete nor uniform in every part
of the country. The ideal of romantic love defiant of antecedents remained attractive. Some individuals stood altogether
apart from the churches, and conversion and "leakage" continued to move communicants from one affiliation to another.
In some places long-standing denominational disputes still
were live issues; and elsewhere differences of language and
custom retained a stubborn importance. None the less, the
three categories of religion increasingly set the terms within
which many men organized their social life.

The older ethnic identifications continued vital, but their
form changed as the number of foreign-born fell, as second
and third generations came of age, and as the problems of
depression gave way to those of war. Questions posed by the

war altered the old nationalism, and the relaxation of tensions eased the necessity for defensive measures. Nevertheless, many Americans still found values in the recollection of their antecedents.

The war first affected Americans in the immediate appeals for relief. The response was generous and united, in accord with the long tradition of aid for overseas distress. Relief Committees operated in behalf of all the allied nations, the English, French, Poles, Czechs, Russians, Dutch, and Jews. Those Americans whom ethnic loyalties endowed with a particular sense of obligation found these activities an important means of demonstrating their solidarity with the beleaguered countries.

But the intense nationalistic overtones of these affiliations did not survive this war. By now, a quarter of a century after the end of free immigration, the personal connections were weaker and new issues often subordinated these loyalties to other considerations.

Some groups faced a direct choice and made it without hesitation. German-Americans after Pearl Harbor saw the incompatibility of support of Hitler with their obligations to the United States; and the Italians who fifteen years earlier had sent their jewelry to be melted for Mussolini's war chest knew their duty and interest lay in fighting him. Likewise, White Russians subordinated their hatred of the Soviets to the need for supporting their adopted country's ally.

Other people made more complicated choices. As one nation after another was invaded and conquered, conflicting governments in exile appealed for support. The Polish-Americans were torn between *Nowy Swiat* and the National Council of Americans of Polish Descent, both hostile to Russia, and the Warsaw group who saw the main enemy in Germany. The Romanians, the Hungarians, the Yugoslavs in the United States were similarly divided.

Ultimately the decisions were not made in nationalistic terms, but in accord with the policy of the State Department. The shift of government support from Mikhailovich to Tito and from the London to the Warsaw Poles was generally accepted; despite die-hard opposition, the election of 1944 showed Roosevelt lost no support in Polish or Slavic districts because of his stand.

The alternatives were clearer still after 1945. The Communist regimes hostile to the United States that assumed power east of the iron curtain could not command the support of any American group, except that of committed Party members. The exposure of the totalitarian character of the Soviet Union destroyed the last vestiges of sympathy for the Party among Americans and alienated all but the most hardened members and fellow travelers. The front organizations in almost all the ethnic groups collapsed; and nationalism was engulfed in the broader question of opposition to totalitarianism.

Where nationalism persisted it occasioned no conflicts with the demands of loyalty to the United States. Through the decade, the Irish-Americans continued to listen to oratory denouncing the British partition of the Island; but they no longer opposed the alliance with England. Jews supported the Zionist demand for a state, but now the necessities for refugee relief outweighed all other considerations. The American defenders of Israel argued it would be a friendly bastion for democracy in the Middle East manned by the victims of Nazism.

Occasionally an excited young man rushed off to enlist — for Britain in the trying days of 1940 and 1941, or for Israel in 1948. But with rare exceptions the mass of Americans thought they could best serve such causes in the armed forces of the United States. Behind the transformation was the fact that patriotism no longer demanded a narrow, exclusive concern with an isolated America; it had become involved, on a basis that Americans of Polish and Irish and Italian and Russian descent could share, in a universal struggle against totalitarianism. That struggle opened the way to a reëxamination of what democracy in the United States meant to all these people.

The defensive aspects of ethnic group action also lost their intensity in this period. The "minorities" were readier than ever to resist anti-Semitism, or anti-Catholicism, or other forms of discrimination. But the substantial gains of the decade — the new opportunities in employment, in education, in equality of housing — and the subsidence of open expression of hostility relieved these defensive activities of the bitterness born of persecution. The persistent fight against surviving inequities was phrased less often in terms of the privileges of particular groups and more often in terms of the rights and objectives of all Americans.

There remained the complex of institutions and societies inherited from the past. The foreign-language press and theater continued to decline in strength and in some places faded away completely. Fraternal societies and philanthropic institutions, schools and churches held on for the services they rendered; and often in the third and fourth generation, Americans still found themselves members of organizations their ancestors had created for reasons no one any longer remembered.

There remained also a will to be identified with those ancestors. At a time when the longing for stability gave roots more importance than ever, men were anxious to know and to show themselves for what they were, not simply out of filiopiety and pride but out of reluctance to conceal any part of a past increasingly important to them as individuals. It became urgent, as a gesture of resistance to all the threats of totalitarianism, to all the pressures toward conformity, that each person reveal within his Americanism the peculiarities of heritage that set him off from his fellows.

It was not as common now for names to be changed; nor was there the former eagerness to pass into the "old" families. Instead, a man was likely to present himself for what he was without pretense or apology. An unyielding world in an age beset with dangers to the individual made so many other demands upon his individuality that he could not in self-respect compromise these signs of his identity.

Furthermore, Americans discovered positive values in the consciousness of their antecedents as soon as they ceased to use their heritage as a means of self-justification and turned back to it for assistance in locating themselves in the twentieth-century world. In the ranks of a society crowded by almost every other force toward likemindedness and conformity, there was a sense of primal personal security in the awareness that men should not suffer for the diversities of their antecedents. If they were free to avow their own ancestors, there was a promise of freedom in their own futures.

Now, as earlier, color made a difference. There were still penalties attached to color; and in some groups it remained an unwanted stigma. Among the Mexicans, for instance, the impulse toward *Mexicanismo*, the pride in the culture of the homeland, clashed with the certainty that their dark skins laid them open to discrimination. Often, it was said, "when the Mexican starts going up, he goes clear out of sight and becomes a good old Southern California family." [2] And it was the same with Puerto Ricans: those who could shed their identity did so.

Yet the experience of the Negroes in this decade showed color itself could be a satisfying mode of identification. The Negro too sensed the stronger pull of the churches; at the end of the decade more than half the 13,000,000 in the United States were active members. But their affiliations were with separate colored institutions. Only half a million were members of "white" denominations; and even these were set off either in independent synods or in segregated churches.

There were some efforts after 1940 to counteract the tendency. Catholics in New York, St. Louis, and elsewhere consciously set about to destroy the old barriers. Interracial Protestant churches appeared in Philadelphia, Detroit, San Francisco, and Washington. And, in 1946, the Federal Council of Churches went on record in favor of "a non-segregated Church and a non-segregated society." [3] But the mass of Negroes remained apart, for their adherence to their own forms involved more than the negative acceptance of a disability thrust on them from without. Most were not willing to surrender the satisfaction of the store-front churches and the Pentecostal sects that continued to sprout in the cities and villages for the sake of admission to communions that other men had formed and led. Their churches were their own and served the Negroes as religious institutions created by others could not.

Negroes were more secure than ever before, and in a better position to defend their claim to equal civil rights. The gains achieved in lowering the bars of Jim Crow did not lull the group into contentment, but rather heightened its determination to carry the battle on. If they could ride unsegregated in interstate railroads and sit with white students in the universities, why not in trolleys and grammar schools?

National consciousness also lingered. As the Japanese marched across Asia after Pearl Harbor, some Negroes harbored a secret satisfaction at the humbling of the whites by colored men. There was some talk of a World Congress of Darker Peoples, an increase in black chauvinism, and a "determination to rid the world of the Caucasian problem." [4]

But recognition in the war and the progressive awareness that a way was opening before them by which a share in America would be theirs softened the old resentments. Pride in the achievements of the group took increasingly another form; color was not the shameful badge of a former servitude but the mark of a common heritage that had made them a part of American society. Their ancestors, they proudly pointed out, had been on the continent longer than those of most other citizens. As the penalties attached to that heritage grew less burdensome, there was less inclination to evade or apolo-

gize for it. "I'm through with passing," many a Negro proclaimed, as the positive qualities of his identification with the
group more frequently outweighed the pains of discrimination. Why wish to be white, asked Ethel Waters? The ebony
standards, she protested, were more pleasing.[5]

Yet, it was still not "fun to be black," as one Negro author
over-optimistically thought to put it. The victims of the Cicero
riots had evidence of the liabilities still attached to their color.
Discrimination in housing, in employment, and in social inter-
course, and other remnants of ancient prejudice continued to
remind the Negro he was not as free as other Americans.
Nonetheless, in the persistent struggle for equality, many colored men were heartened by the distance they had come,
decade by decade since 1900, and at an ever-accelerating pace.
Lynchings had disappeared. Equal political, educational, and
economic rights, still an achievement for the future, now
seemed achievable. For whites everywhere were coming quiet-
ly to recognize the inevitable trend toward a future unmarred
by the old inequalities. How far in the future remained a question. But even while American Negroes burned with indigna-
tion at the news of developments in Malan's South Africa, they
were struck by the contrast with the direction of policy in
their own country.*

In a decade of the world at war, the prolonged crisis had
summoned up hidden resources and led Americans to closer
self-awareness. The recollection of diverse antecedents, religious differences, even color — to which so many penalties
had once been attached — thus became the points about which
the ethnic groups could, with a sense of individual dignity,
reorder their lives.

* While this book was in press, the decision of the Supreme Court in the
case of *Brown* v. *Board of Education*, in May 1954, in principle abolished
segregation in public education and confirmed the unmistakable trend in
policy.

CHAPTER X

Group Life in America

The half century had opened upon a nation jubilant in the aftermath of the splendid little war against Spain; it closed upon a people tired of a decade of indecisive conflict. Unexpected war, unhappy peace, depression, and war again had sorely tried men's capacity for endurance. The old optimistic certainties had not survived the trial. The mood of the early 1950's was one of hope, but not of confidence.

Their history had, however, left Americans with critical resources of resiliency. They had been gathered together from a multitude of sources; and the long course of expansion together with the free structure of their society permitted them to evolve ways of acting in voluntary groups that reflected the diversity of their origins. The booming growth of the country at the turn of the century left room for many differences; the abstinence of government made many important areas of action the concern of private associations.

Occasional signs of strain had been the price of freedom in this society, a consequence of mobility and the lack of controls. Now and again some of the groups had stood in open antagonism — Know-Nothing against Catholic, Klansman against Negro, Kearneyite against Chinese. Each time, renewal of expansive energies and the country's immense opportunities had resolved the conflict.

The First World War was the start of drastic change. The scope of government widened to take in many areas once the province of private action; and patriotism generated a narrow restrictive nationalism, intolerant of differences, and attached to the rising power of the political state. The end of immigration shortly thereafter, and then the depression convinced many Americans that the era of expansion was over. The fear that resources and opportunities were dwindling left in their minds no room for inefficient diversities. Bitter conflicts ensued.

The effects of the second war, in this respect, were different. The crisis revealed unexpected capacities for further economic and social expansion; and nationalism, though more demanding of conformity, lost its exclusive character. Tension eased, and as men sought the reassurance of stable personal lives in a chaotic world they found new values in their ethnic affiliations.

For the groups themselves changed. Their voluntary character left them fluid and adaptable to the forms of a swiftly moving society as well as to the changing needs of their members. The complex of associations and activities through which the individual acted shifted in response to the new conditions. Yet the groupings retained an ethnic quality. For when men felt no compulsion to deny their origins and were free to make choices without penalties, they formed friendships and marriages, worshipped and read, within a pattern of life molded by their antecedents.

These were not hard-and-fast divisions that set men off on islands from which they could not cross. These were rather overlapping boundaries on a mainland, so that one man could stand at once in several different fields. In this society, furthermore, broad areas remained open in which individuals acted without reference to ethnic affiliations. The neighborhood, the union, the service club, the professional association, and the political party drew people together as participants in other kinds of activities, and created other kinds of meaningful social interests and distinctions. What men were by trade and party influenced and was influenced by their ethnic connections. But the open areas of social action kept the ethnic group from becoming a prison within which they were locked and left it a fortress from which they could draw strength.

At mid-century such groups were more significant than ever. The United States, like the rest of the world, then confronted the problem of safeguarding the individual against the overwhelming power of the state. The techniques of control had become so effective and the limits of its functions so wide, that government, massive and impersonal, was in the position to crush the individual by its demand for unwavering obedience, total loyalty, and absolute uniformity. Only through the action of non-political, voluntary associations could men check the state's power without directly opposing it. As long as men are free so to act, they cannot be reduced to the blankness of the subjects of the totalitarian regimes.

Such associations in many nations, including the United States, were called into being by regional, professional, cultural, and occupational differences. But in America, they were as well the products of ethnic diversities, reaching across the generations from the past, and adding richness and strength to its democratic way of life.

Never was the strength more needed. Americans moved into the perilous second half of the century without the least assurance that they approached the end of a conflict, exorbitantly expensive in lives and human energies. The oppressive demands of the struggle closed in on them from every side, so that they could hope for stability only in orderly personal relationships. The sense of belonging to a group with its roots in the past helped create that order. To the extent that such groups were fluid and unrestrictive, they held men's loyalties, without limiting their opportunities, and steadied them for the shocks of an uncertain future.

NOTES

Foreword

1. Oscar Handlin, *This Was America* (Cambridge, 1949), 230.

Chapter II — The Color Line

1. Edward A. Pollard, *The Lost Cause Regained* (New York, 1868), 14.
2. Stetson Kennedy, "3.2 Democracy in the South," *Survey Graphic*, May, 1944.
3. Booker T. Washington, *Selected Speeches* (E. D. Washington, ed., Garden City, 1932), 34.
4. Alfred Holt Stone, *Mississippi Constitution* (Oxford, Miss., 1901), 161–162, 166, 167.
5. *The Negro in Virginia*. Compiled by Writers' Program of the W.P.A. (New York, 1940), 293.
6. W. E. B. DuBois, "My Evolving Program for Negro Freedom," R. W. Logan, ed., *What the Negro Wants* (Chapel Hill, 1944), 36.
7. *Harper's Weekly*, Dec. 1, 1905, p. 1699.
8. J. F. Steiner, *Japanese Invasion* (Chicago, 1917), 143.
9. Eliot Grinnell Mears, *Resident Orientals on the American Pacific Coast* (Chicago, 1928), 146.
10. D'Arcy McNickle, *They Came Here First* (Philadelphia, 1949), 263.
11. Angie Debo, *And Still the Waters Run* (Norman, 1940), 11–17, 20–23.

Chapter III — The Migrations

1. Jacques Ducharme, *The Shadows of the Trees* (New York, 1943), 64.
2. James H. Kennedy, *History of the Ohio Society of New York, 1885–1905* (New York, 1906), 18.

CHAPTER IV — THE STRAINS OF A FREE SOCIETY

1. *Survey*, Nov. 6, 1909, p. 168.
2. *Boston Transcript*, Dec. 29, 1906.
3. *Boston Morning Globe*, Sept. 25, 1914.
4. *Boston Record*, March 16, 1896.
5. Prescott Hall Collection (Harvard College Library), X, 137.
6. Francis A. Walker, "Restriction of Immigration," *Atlantic Monthly*, LXXVII (1896), 828.
7. Prescott Hall Collection, X, 77.
8. *Ibid.*, IX, 13; *Helena Record*, March 12, 1908.
9. Prescott Hall Collection, II, 127 ff.
10. *Milwaukee Journal*, Feb. 16, 1897.
11. *Boston Transcript*, Dec. 29, 1906; Prescott Hall Collection, IX (March 8, 1909).

CHAPTER V — WORLD WAR

1. Atlantic Union, *Annual Report for 1906*, 20.
2. *New York Times*, March 5, 1916, p. 7:1.
3. Emil Lengyel, *Americans from Hungary* (Philadelphia, 1948), 184.
4. E. F. Kinkead to Wilson, May 27, 1918, in Alden Jamison, "Irish-Americans, the Irish Question, and American Diplomacy" (Harvard University Archives), 614.
5. Woodrow Wilson, *President Wilson's Addresses* (G. M. Harper, ed., New York, 1918), 150; Burton J. Hendrick, *Life and Letters of Walter H. Page* (New York, 1924), II, 144.
6. Governor James M. Cox of Ohio, in Carl Wittke, *German-Americans and the World War* (Columbus, 1936), 181.
7. Bohemian National Alliance in *Literary Digest*, LIV (June 23, 1917), 20.
8. *Literary Digest*, May 25, 1918, p. 32.
9. David Philipson, *Centenary Papers and Others* (Cincinnati, 1919), 58.
10. Reprinted in *Negro Year Book* (1918–19) from *Crusader Magazine*.
11. *Amsterdam News* (New York), in *Negro Year Book* (1918–19), 100.
12. R. C. Simmons, quoted *ibid.*, 45.

CHAPTER VI — POSTWAR ERA

1. Quoted *Literary Digest*, Nov. 30, 1918, p. 8.
2. Jamison, "Irish-Americans and American Diplomacy," 651.
3. *Foreign Born*, Nov., 1920, p. 8.
4. *Literary Digest*, Nov. 8, 1919.

5. *Literary Digest*, Sept. 1, 1917, p. 9.
6. *Literary Digest*, Mar. 8, 1918, pp. 92 ff.
7. *Literary Digest*, Nov. 22, 1919, p. 15.
8. F. Scott Fitzgerald, *The Beautiful and the Damned* (New York, 1926), 283.
9. Michael Williams, *Shadow of the Pope* (New York, 1932), 189.

CHAPTER VIII — NEW PATTERNS OF ACTION

1. *La Voce del popolo italiano*, Apr. 2, 1937, *Annals of Cleveland, Newspaper Series*, 1937, II.
2. *Ibid.*, Mar. 19, 1937.
3. *Opportunity*, Aug., 1935, p. 230.
4. Sara Harris, *Father Divine, Holy Husband* (New York, 1953), 177.

CHAPTER IX — A DECADE OF GLOBAL WAR

1. D. A. Wilkerson, "Freedom — Through Victory in War and Peace," Logan, *What the Negro Wants*, 198.
2. Beatrice Griffith, *American Me* (Boston, 1948), 229, 230.
3. Liston Pope, "Caste in the Church," *Survey Graphic* (Jan., 1947), 104.
4. G. S. Schuyler, "The Caucasian Problem," Logan, *What the Negro Wants*, 286.
5. "I'm Through with Passing," *Ebony*, March, 1951.

INDEX

Abie's Irish Rose, 161
Acadians, 85, 160
Adams, Henry, 3
Adams, J. Q., 99
Adams family, 100
Adana, 66
Africa, Negroes and, 34
Afro-American, 29
Afro-American Council, 34
Afro-Americans, 134
Agricultural Adjustment Act, 176
Agriculture: development, 4, 7, 15, 143, 157, 165, 175, 208; immigrants and, 9, 40, 57; Southern, 19, 83; Southwestern, 53, 110
Alabama, 22, 133, 176
Albania, 129
Albanians, 66, 67, 119, 141, 142, 191
Aldrich, N. W., 99
Alger, Horatio, 12
Alianza-Hispano-Americano, 159
Alliance College, 69
Alliance of Polish Literary Circles, 188
Amana, 85
America First, 212
American Association for Recognition of Irish Republic, 139
American Defense Society, 124
American Federation of Labor, 39, 89, 102, 144, 203
American Hungarian Loyalty League, 129
American Jewish Committee, 74, 132, 140, 141, 201
American Jewish Congress, 132, 140, 141, 192, 201
American Legion, 146, 198
American Museum Natural History, 152
American Protective Association, 80, 92, 103, 117, 147, 179
American Protective League, 124
American Scandinavian Foundation, 77
Ameryka-Echo, 129
Amish, 85
Amsterdam News, 29
Anarchism, 60, 145, 148
Ancient Order of Foresters, 52, 79
Ancient Order of Hibernians, 116
Anglo-Saxons, 80, 100, 101, 114
Anti-Catholicism, 80, 91, 103, 150, 151, 152, 179, 218
Anti-Defamation League, 201
Anti-Semitism, 103, 117, 118, 150, 152, 179, 192, 201, 218

Arabs, 43, 67
Arizona, 53, 110
Arkansas, 17
Armenian Benevolent Union, 66
Armenians, 43, 66, 87, 88, 104, 119, 130, 138
Arrighi, Antonio, 59
Article X, 139
Aryan race, 102, 152
Association Canada-Américaine, 52
Associations, viii, 41, 51, 92, 173
Assyrian immigrants, 66
Athens, Archbishop of, 64
Atlanta, 22, 35, 83
Atlantic islands, 62
Atlantic Union, 115
Atlantis, 65
Attucks, Crispus, 160
Austria, 8, 11, 70, 118, 119, 127, 128, 151
Autocephalous Albanian Church, 67
Azores, 62, 63

Balfour Declaration, 131, 141, 161, 192
Baltimore, 19
Bellamy, Edward, 5
Bellingham, Wash., 42
Beneš, Eduard, 128
Beneš, Voyta, 128
Berea College Case, 25
Bermuda Conference, 171
Biddeford, Maine, 49
Bilmanis, Alexander, 129
Birmingham, 83, 208
Birth rate, 6, 156, 211
Bismarck, Otto, 116, 118
Black Hand, 103
Black Legion, 185, 221
Bohemian National Alliance, 127
Bolsheviks, 145, 150
Bosnian immigrants, 67
Boston: Brahmins, 85; immigrants in, 57, 59, 63, 65, 67, 72; Negroes, 19, 133; politics, 93
Boston Guardian, 34
Boston Transcript, 98, 188
Brahmins, 85, 100, 188, 189
Brandeis, Louis D., 131
Bravas, 63
Bread v. *Rice*, 39
Bremer, Fredrika, viii
British-American Association, 80
British immigrants, 78ff., 87, 89, 96, 115, 117, 156

238   *INDEX*

INDEX

DATE DUE

APR 6 '66			
APR 1 0 '68			
May 6			
APR 4 '70			
DEC 8 71			
APR 1 6 74			
FEB 2 1 '84			
MAY 4 '87			
GAYLORD			PRINTED IN U.S.A